# of an Tao Uncluttered Life

Karen Hicks

The Tao of an Uncluttered Life

Lao Tzu's Ten Principles for Organization.

HUMANICS TRADE GROUP
Atlanta, Frankfurt, Paris

The Tao of an Uncluttered Life

A Humanics Trade Group Publication

Humanics Limited,
P.O. Box 7400,
Atlanta, GA 30357
www.humanicspub.com

Printed in the United States of America

Library of Congress Preassigned Card Number: 99-63966
ISBN 0-89334-293-9

Dedication

I dedicate this book to the following people:

Steve Allen, for planting the thought, then prodding and encouraging me until it became reality.

Mrs. Lillie Carlson, my high school English and Latin teacher, for seeing my potential as a writer before I did and for teaching me how to put my thoughts on paper.

My employers, co-workers, family, and friends including my sisterhood-Betty, Peggy, Twyla, Lee, Shannon, Charli, Andrea, Nan, Vicki, and Wolfwoman Sue-for giving me pleasure and helping me grow.

And, especially, my son Jon, for making it all worthwhile.

*Do that
which consists in taking no action;
Pursue that
which is not meddlesome;
Savour that
which has no flavour.*

Table of Contents

When the best student
hears about The Way
He practices it assiduously;
When the average student
hears about The Way
It seems to him
one moment there and gone the next;
When the worst student
hears about The Way
He laughs out loud.
If he did not laugh
It would be unworthy
of being The Way.

換

Foreword

BY STEVE ALLEN

One of the questions I am most frequently asked is: How are you able to be active in such a variety of professional fields and to produce such a volume of work?

First of all, perhaps I should note that there is nothing of conceit or pride in reporting such a question since it is quite possible to turn out a great amount of material, none of which is high quality. But when others praise my efficiency, they are usually referring to the sort of unexamined system by means of which I professionally operate. My techniques for producing a good deal of creative work is largely a matter of playing-it-by-ear, which happens to be the way I play the piano, though I have no doubt that it would be wise if, in addition to being so naturally prolific, I could consider my creative work as part of a conscious, formal technique. This is what Ms. Hicks has done as regards efficiency and organization.

When she applied for a position on my staff—in 1988—she brought with her several letters of recommendation from which I quote below:

*"She processes written material efficiently, accurately, and with considerable thought. It is no exaggeration whatsoever to state that she did the work of two to three competent and motivated individuals." (Nicholas Sieveking, Ph.D.)

*"Karen proved herself to be a remarkably organized, resourceful and honest individual." (Kenneth Anchor, Ph.D.)

*"While in her position as HUD supervisor, Karen reorganized the department and had it operating in a greatly improved manner. Systems and files have been established that expedite the handling of paperwork." (Joycelyn Hinkle, NCHP Property Management)

*"While in our employment, Karen worked directly under me, performing the work of one and one-half girls. But this was still not enough work to keep her busy. . . . Before I could finish telling her what the project was to be, she already had figured out in her mind how she was going to present it."(Larry Beyreis, Industrial Engineer)

*"Karen's forte is untangling messes and setting up systems. If you need an organizer, she's it. . . . She has performed two full-time jobs at once."(Patricia Warhol, Target Stores, Inc., Advertising Services)

That was enough for me. I hired her on the spot. And I have not been disappointed.

One day, after Karen had completely reorganized our files and created systems that allow even the enormous volume of paperwork that floods my office to flow smoothly, I suggested that she consider writing a book to share her secrets with others. *The Tao of an Uncluttered Life* is the result.

Most manuals about efficiency concentrate either on"rules"to be memorized and followed, or generalized examples of how to be organized at work or in your home. Karen's approach to the subject is much broader. She does give us ten—well, she calls them suggestions rather than rules, since she believes that each person must adapt the general principles to fit his or her own particular lifestyle. But she also presents detailed, step-by-step procedures which show how these recommendations can be applied in the home, on the job and even in our leisure time.

By presenting the material in an easy-to-read-and-understand manner, she gives us a book that is not only enjoyable to study, but one from which anyone could profit. She touches on the importance of using our common sense—our reasoning skills—to alter systems to work for us, and sprinkled throughout the manuscript are quips that provoke thought and encourage an attitude conducive to an organized life.

The Tao of an Uncluttered Life is not heavy-handed. It is Ms. Hicks's contention that the importance of being organized is to enable us to enjoy life itself more. Her final suggestion—"Relax . . . Have Fun"— reinforces this belief. This is a book you will want to refer to often and share with your friends.

The way
that can be spoken of
Is not the constant way; . . .
Hence
always rid yourself of desires
in order to observe [The Way's] secrets;
But always
allow yourself to have desires
in order to observe [Tao's] manifestations.
These two are the same.

A note from the author

Dear Friend,

Tao (rhymes with now) is the universal force within each of us that produces harmony with nature. The ancient Chinese philosophy Taoism is The Way, or course, in all aspects of life that is most effective, least conspicuous and that is in practical and spiritual harmony with nature and the universe. It is the essence of "not doing" to accomplish the greatest good of one's life.

Another Eastern philosophy, Feng Shui (pronounce Fung Shway) puts forth the belief that clutter damages your chi (chee, your life force) and saps your energy.

This book blends these two ancient wisdoms to present ten practical principles to unclutter our lives and bring us into harmony with the natural order of all things. These principles are not meant as rules but rather as suggestions to stimulate and inspire you to uncover the Tao that is within you so that you can regain the vitality you were created to enjoy.

To begin, let's combine two modern-day, Western beliefs and use them to improve our lives. The first is, "If you act as if, then you will be," and the second is, "If you do something in the same way for twenty-one days, it becomes a habit." First, read the book in its entirety. It is short and no-nonsense, because organized people go straight to the bottom line. At the end, you will find two affirmations and a list of the ten organizational principles covered in the book. Make a copy of this page and tape it up where you will see it several times a day. Make a reduced copy to carry in your wallet. If possible, put one up on the job.

Now, for the next twenty-one days, when you first wake up each morning, repeat aloud the morning affirmation: "Today I act efficiently." Say it again-with determination. Again—with promise. Again—with excitement! Say it one last time—with a smile. Throughout the day, let the ten principles guide you in everything you do. When you go to bed at night, say aloud the evening affirmation: "Today I acted efficiently. Tomorrow I will be even more organized."

At the end of twenty-one days, I believe that your life will flow more smoothly, that your energy will increase, and that you will smile more often.

P. S. Because of the current focus on the politically correct use of gender references and the awkwardness of using "he or she" and "him or her," I have coined two words I will use instead throughout the book. (I don't know why no one has done this before.)

Sheh (rhymes with way) will refer to either gender in place of the commonly used "he or she".

Hir (pronounced here) will replace "him or her".

I hope this will make the text flow a bit more smoothly and avoid ruffling anyone's sensibilities. Who knows, maybe the words will catch on!

In his every movement
a man of great virtue
Follows The Way
and The Way only.
As a thing The Way is
Shadowy, indistinct.
Indistinct and shadowy,
Yet within it is an image.
Shadowy and indistinct,
Yet within it is a substance.
Dim and dark,
Yet within it is an essence.
This essence is quite genuine
And within it
is something that can be
tested.

*Anticipate
possibilities,
enjoy
realities.*

Principle One: Imagine

If you don't know what you want, you'll never get it. If you don't know where you're going, you'll never get there. You were created to be and do anything you can imagine. The more details you envision, the more closely you'll achieve your ideal. Being organized means reaching your objective by the most direct route. Imagination can show you The Way in everything you wish to accomplish, from the big picture of your life's goals to the minutia of your daily tasks.

Life Goals

To visualize (imagine) a personal/career goal, sit down in a quiet place and daydream about where you would like to be and what you would be doing if you were living the perfect life. Write out your schedule for a typical day spent completely happy, answering the standard reporter questions of WHO, WHAT, WHERE, WHEN, and HOW.

* What will you look like? What will you wear? Where will you get out of bed? What is your view of the outside world—physically, spiritually and financially?

* What is the first thing you will do in the morning? How does that shower feel streaming down upon your body? How does your breakfast taste?

* Who will be in your day? How will you spend your work time? How will you spend your playtime? How will you feed your spiritual self?

As you picture your day, write down the answers to these questions, and any others that you can think of. But don't just list the answers, pretend the day was yesterday and you're writing about it in your diary or journal, or in a letter to a friend. Describe the colors, smells, tastes, sounds and touch of every single minute, as well as your feelings.

Once you have this information clearly in focus, you will be able to judge every action of every day as to its ability to bring you closer to that visualized future day. If you choose those actions that move you forward most directly, you will have an organized plan for achieving your goal.

Even if you never consciously follow any of the ten principles put forth in this book, if you write out every detail you imagine about your ideal life and accept that this life can be yours, you will know the bliss of its manifestation.

Daily Tasks

It may not be as exciting as visualizing your perfect life, but imagining also works in planning daily tasks. Here's the chance for each of us to be an actor. Think of the most organized person you know. Now pretend you're that person. Imagine how sheh would complete the task at hand and act as sheh would act.

If you're writing a letter, memo, or instruction, imagine you are the recipient. Play out the role: What is your first impression of the document? Is it neat? Is it easy to read? Is it broken into short paragraphs? Do you understand the message? How do you feel while reading it? What response will the document elicit?

Another example of how imagining can work in your daily tasks is, for example, preparing a trouble-free travel itinerary. If this is something you do frequently, you will save time and ensure completeness if you make up a master form to be used for each trip. To create the form (or to plan a one-time trip), imagine every minute, from leaving the house until returning again. As you envision the trip in your head, write down every question that could conceivably cross you mind and follow it with a blank space for writing down the answer:

Is my car road-ready? If not, what do I need to do to make it so?
Do I have maps or directions to every place I need to go?
How am I getting to the airport, bus or train station?

What time do I have to leave?

What airline, train or bus do I take?

When do I arrive at my destination?

Once I arrive, how will I get to where I'm staying? If being met by someone, where will we meet?

If staying in a hotel, what is the name, phone number and reservation information?

What will I want when I get to my room that can be requested when making the reservation (e.g., fruit, a wet bar with extra scotch or juice instead of alcohol, a robe, extra towels)?

What am I supposed to do in each city I visit? (Here leave several additional blank lines on which to fill in the activities for each trip. Under each activity list the famous five questions "who, what, where, when, and how"). Make sure you leave blank lines after each question for your answers.

What date and time do I leave for home?

How am I getting home? What route will I take if driving or what public transportation information do I need?

How am I getting to the airport, bus or train station?

If using public transportation, when do I arrive at my hometown station and how will I get to my house from there?

Once you have the form as a worksheet, you simply have to imagine each specific trip and fill in the answers to the questions. As you encounter questions that involve other people, call and confirm arrangements with those persons.

Life being what it is, you should also consider problems that could arise and jot down solutions:

What if the arranged ground transportation is not at the airport?

Whom do I call?

Is there a confirmation number for the order?

Who hired the driver?

What is the name of the person who took the reservation?

If maps are used, highlight the route. Auto clubs and state tourism bureaus are good sources for out-of-town maps. Keep those frequently used on hand, or use one of the online mapsites.

In addition to maps, write out a little crib sheet on a Post-it note. Here's an example: Take Highway 134 West from Burbank to 110 South to

10 West. Go approximately 55 miles and exit at Palm Springs Road, go six blocks and turn left at Sunshine Lane.

It can also be helpful, when writing up directions, to note an exit or landmark just before your scheduled turn and one just after your scheduled turn. This way you will know when to prepare to turn or when you have gone too far. Stick the note on your dashboard for easy referral.

If your situation requires a formal itinerary, you can easily transfer the information from the working form to the standard format.

Imagining is the first key to being organized in every area of your life. Imagine your day tomorrow. See yourself being calm, organized, and happy. Visualize doing your taxes with no hassle. Imagine cleaning your house; asking for a raise; deciding on a college; buying a summer home; successfully completing every daily activity. See the big smile on your face and the twinkle in your eye. Soon you'll be experiencing them for real.

My schedule for an ideal day:

_____

_____

_____

_____

_____

_____

_____

_____

_____

_____

Lay plans
for the
accomplishment of the difficult
Before it becomes difficult;
Make something big
By starting with it
when small.
Difficult things in the world
Must needs have their beginnings
in the easy;
Big things
must needs have their beginnings
In the small.

*Know
your worth
and
deliver it.*

Principle Two: Plan Ahead

Planning ahead is important for several reasons: It gives value to one's actions; instills confidence to act boldly; increases the motivation to complete the necessary work; and, most importantly, relieves the stress of day-to-day life. Additionally, if you plan ahead, you will generally be more apt to do things right the first time and thereby avoid the extra moments and effort to do them over. This all adds up to a fun, smooth-running day where things get accomplished and success is born.

Imagining is the first step to planning ahead, but there are also more pragmatic actions that fall into this category that will help you complete a task more quickly and easily—more efficiently.

Develop Your Database

One way to plan ahead for life in general is to create a database in your brain. This is because, as every schoolchild knows, the more information you are given to solve a problem, the faster and easier it is to solve it. There are many ways to expand overall knowledge: taking classes, attending seminars and workshops, reading, using audio and visual aids, surfing the net, and conversing with others, to name a few.

But it takes more than just having the know-how. We must also have common sense. We must learn how to think. There are several good books and tapes available on the process of reasoning, including Steve

Allen's *Dumbth: And 81 Ways to Make Americans Smarter* (Prometheus Books, Buffalo, NY, 1989). They deserve our attention. With this foundation of facts and common sense, you'll be able to plan ahead to save time in every area of your life.

Make the Most of Downtime

Use slow times to prepare for the busy times. For instance, if you're a food server, do your sidework. Restock glasses and dishes, backup supplies, make coffee, fill condiment holders, etc. even if those things are not your assigned tasks. Would you rather hope someone else does it, or have the items available when you get slammed? In an office, restock the supplies at your desk, delete computer files no longer needed, make forms to streamline tasks, clean out your files, contemplate ways to arrange your work area more efficiently. In a factory, clean your workspace. At home, keep extra batteries, candles, staple food items, etc. on hand.

Use Lists

An easy way to plan ahead for your shopping tasks is to compile a list as you go. I use a piece of scratch paper held to my refrigerator by a colorful magnet (HINT: Use the back sides of paper cut into uniform pieces for scratch paper. It helps the pocketbook and the planet.) When I first notice something is getting low, or when I open the last item in my supply, I immediately make a note on the paper, which is then used as my shopping list. You may keep your list in a drawer, or on a bulletin board. The important thing is to keep it handy for use.

This ongoing list is even more important if you have a large family, each member of which is constantly depleting your supply. Elicit their help in jotting down things needed to lessen the chance of forgetting something. On shopping day, simply add any last-minute items, and you're off to the market.

If you use coupons (see Principle #5), keep them close to the shopping list—in a small envelope or one of those organized coupon wallets tabbed for the different types of purchases. (HINT: Be sure to go through your coupons at least once a month and discard those that have expired.) Once your shopping list is compiled, flip through the coupons with the list in front of you, pulling out those you can use this trip. Write the coupon brand and amount in brackets after the listed item. Other brands may be a better buy, despite the coupon, and having this information on your list saves you from fumbling through the coupons at the store to price compare or to remember what brand you have a coupon for. You can also code each item by department—P for produce, M for meat, etc.—for easy spotting when you're in that particular area of the store.

There are also preprinted shopping lists available. If you regularly purchase the items listed, they're a great aid to planning ahead. Or you can type up your own standard list, sorting it into groups in the same order as your favorite market's sections. After each item, type the brand and quantity usually purchased, and in front of each item, leave a five-space blank line for checking off items to be replenished. Add a few blank lines at the bottom for special items. Photocopy or print off several copies of this handmade list and hang them on a clipboard in the pantry. Everyone's lifestyle may require a slightly different twist on the details, but the basic technique of planning ahead applies.

Lists also apply to office shopping. If you're the person in charge of keeping the supply cabinets stocked, type up a list of every item kept on hand. Include the stock number, the quantity of items in a unit (i.e., manila folders come in boxes of twenty-five, so if you want fifty folders, you would purchase two units). Add a five-space line in front of each item for entering a checkmark or quantity. Post the sheet on the door of the supply cabinet or room and ask each employee who notices that something is getting low to check off the item. Add a few blank lines at the bottom of the list for any special supplies an employee might need. If you call in your order, put the phone number of your office supply company at the top of the page, as well as your company's account number. You also might want to note the catalog page number by each item, in case you have to refer to it. This system organizes—and thereby shortens—the processes of ordering, verifying delivery, and updating your inventory.

Carry a small notebook with you (or an index card or scratch paper) on which are listed items you want to purchase but have no deadline for obtaining—a pair of cowboy boots, a new bookcase (include dimensions), a picture frame (again with the size noted). Carry a small measuring tape on your key chain, or in your purse or pocket. With this planning ahead, the necessary information is readily available if you run

9

across the item on sale, or you get an unexpected bonus and want to spend the extra money judiciously.

This is an especially great tip if you're a garage-sale addict like I am. I recently completed a large jigsaw puzzle that I glued in order to keep. I knew that to frame it commercially would cost more than fifty dollars. But the weekend after I had noted the size information to carry with me, I was able to buy the perfect frame at a garage sale for eight dollars.

You can use lists in many other areas as well. List your stops in order on a Post-it note before you leave to run errands and you can plan them so you can make a big circle, saving time, stress and money. This also helps you not to forget an important stop.

As we will cover in Principle #4, lists can even be helpful in reaching your life goals. By listing everything you must do to achieve your ideal life, you will have a roadmap of how to get there.

Plan Ahead for Taxes

Saving your receipts on deductible items (see Principle #3) can ease the pain of tax preparation. Be sure to note on entertainment receipts the names of persons involved and what was discussed. You need this information to claim the deduction, and if you write it down as it occurs, you won't have to try to remember whom you took to lunch one Tuesday in June and why when you are rushing to beat the April 15 deadline or trying to save the deduction in an audit. Advanced planning of remodeling tasks, major business purchases, and investments can also help you receive maximum tax advantages.

Do a Trial Run

If you're trying out a new recipe, first read the instructions all the way through, setting out each utensil and ingredient that you will need. Now you're ready to begin. (HINT: Put away each item as soon as you finish using it. Relieving the counter-clutter as you go will make the baking process more efficient and keep the cleanup from being a major task.)

If you're assembling a new piece of furniture or a toy, again begin by reading the instruction sheet completely. Now gather all the tools and supplies you'll need.

Lay out the unit's parts, sorting into piles of like items. Use a large tray or the long side of the packing box to hold the piles of screws, nails and other small pieces. Check each part against the list provided on the instruction sheet and label each with a Post-it note as identified by the manufacturer—shelf C, leveler bracket, assembly screw H, etc. Don't neglect this important step. While it may seem to take more time, I guarantee it will make the task much more stress-free and enjoyable. It will also save you from getting the item almost together and then finding out that you are missing a part. It is much easier to stack the unassembled pieces out of the way until the missing part arrives than to store a partially together bulky piece of furniture.

The next step before beginning to assemble something is to visualize the finished project, holding up the various parts as they will fit together to be sure you have the finished fronts all facing front, the predrilled holes in the right spots, that sort of thing. If you have ever goofed on this, as I have, you know the importance of this.

If you're sewing, lay out all the pieces before you pin the pattern down. Imagine the pieces sewn together. Do the patterns match? Is the nap going in the right direction?

If you're preparing a report, essay, or other written material, do an outline of the document, noting points to be covered in each section. This will keep you on track. Even better, you can kick back with a glass of wine or soda while you prepare the outline. As your creative juices flow, the outline will capture every insightful point you want to make so you won't forget to make it.

Do Your Research

The first day on a new office job, go through all the files that pertain to your job description, even if you have to do it on your lunch break. This not only gives you a good overview of your responsibilities, but by familiarizing yourself with where things are filed at the onset, you won't have to fumble around looking for items you are asked for when you are on your own.

If you work for a large company or a factory, visit other departments. See how your department fits into the entire organization (see Principle #7). If you want your employer to purchase new equipment to streamline your workload, research the costs and pluses and minuses of each alternative. Type up a short, itemized proposal. Your request will get a much faster—and probably more favorable—response. This also works well for convincing your employer that you deserve a raise (see Principle #4).

If you move into a new home, explore every room, closet and shelf and visualize your belongings in place, before you unpack. Sometimes it is helpful to draw a rough, to-scale diagram of the floor plan and cut out to-scale shapes to represent your large items. It's a lot easier to shuffle paper sofas and bureaus than the real thing.

Plan for Obstacles

The universe seems to have a cosmic sense of humor and occasionally allows even the best-laid plans to hit an obstacle. The Tao of dealing with obstacles is much like that of a river that encounters land in its path. If it can't flow around the obstacle, it moves off in another direction. If that is impossible, the river pauses, gathers its strength, and with gentle but firm persistence, eventually erodes away the land that blocks it.

In the same way, don't let obstacles to your goal throw you. Try to see them as opportunities to test your mettle and build your desire for your chosen dream. Have a plan B. But if, after exploring all your alternatives, no forward movement is possible, pause and enjoy the moment of rest as you gather your strength for a new assault.

Plan for Death

Even though we don't like to discuss—or even think about—the subject of death, planning ahead for this inevitable event is the kindest action you can take for your family. *In the Checklist of Life* by Lynn and Martin McPhelimy (A.A.I.P. Publishing Company, LLC, 1997) is a marvelous workbook that will not only make the procedure simple and painless but provide a wonderful keepsake for your future generations. I urge every adult to purchase this book and fill in the blanks.

Plan Something Fun

Now that you are committed to planning ahead in every area of your life, throw a celebration. Planning ahead will turn the party into an event.

Once the invitations are sent, the first thing you must do to ensure a successful, stress-free party is to choose your menu carefully. Select items that can be prepared ahead and require only minimal last-minute attention. Visualize your guests eating the food. Is there an appealing blend of colors, textures and flavors? Once your menu is selected, make your shopping list with your recipes in front of you so you don't forget an important ingredient.

Serve hors d'oeuvres that are easy to handle. If your guests are juggling a plate and drink, will they be able to eat something that requires two hands? How messy will the item be to eat while walking and talking? Something may look good and taste good, but if it is awkward to eat while mingling, the item will not be popular. Have you ever been to a catered party and wondered where to dispose of buffalo wing bones or chicken skewers? Spare your guests the trauma and yourself the cleanup time required to find all the stashing places people put such items by making arrangements for convenient disposal of waste. If you're short on trashcans, use boxes covered with fancy paper, tinfoil or newspaper comic pages and line them with trash bags. (HINT: Use two trash bags, one inside the other, to prevent leaking of even the most liquid garbage.)

Setting up a multilevel buffet like you see at catered parties is an easy and attractive way to serve your food. All you need are tablecloths or sheets, books, boxes or pieces of Styrofoam to create eye-appealing levels, and decorative items to jazz up your table: flowers or floral greens, bunches of kale, fresh fruit or vegetables, marbles, smooth stones, glitter, peanuts-whatever fits the theme of your party.

Visualize your guests going through the buffet line and set up your food so it will be pleasing to the eye and keep the lines moving efficiently: plates first, then the food (cold, then warm) and lastly, the silverware and napkins. Decide on serving dishes and utensils. Are there items you must rent or borrow, such as chafing dishes to keep hot food hot? Baskets are wonderful for attractive placement of silverware or napkins, and, tipped on the side, can hold rolls and bread, which cascade artistically onto the table. Trays, lazy Susan's or clean, scrap pieces of marble are excellent for serving crudité (raw vegetables), fresh fruit, antipasto or cheese and crackers. Be creative—this is the fun part. Your buffet can be set up the night before the party, with serving dishes and utensils in place, ready for the food. Cover with a sheet to keep off the dust and when you're ready to serve, it will be a breeze.

The best thing about planning ahead for a party is that when the guests arrive, you are free to enjoy their company.

These few examples demonstrate the basic steps to planning ahead that can be applied in everything you do. Having the facts, foreseeing obstacles, and mapping out your plan of action is the secret to being organized.

My plans for my next gathering:

_____

_____

_____

_____

_____

_____

_____

_____

_____

_____

_____

The Way is broad,
reaching left
as well as right . . .
It accomplishes its task
yet lays claim to no merit . . .
It is because
it never attempts
itself to be great
that it succeeds
in becoming great.

Principle Three:
Keep Things Simple

The most essential element of any system you set up is simplicity. If a procedure is easy to remember and execute, you'll be more apt to use it. Therefore it's important that you take every suggestion offered on these pages-or anywhere else for that matter-and adapt them to work for you.

Mrs. Lillie Carlson, my high school English teacher and first mentor, taught me one of the most important principles of writing: In order to break a rule of grammar, punctuation, or structure effectively, you must first know the rule. The same is true about being organized. Once you've studied these suggestions and others, use your common sense to decide on your own course of action.

The only reason to be more organized is to live a happier life, right? Remember . . . it's an attitude. The goal is a smooth-flowing, bottom-line lifestyle. So make it fun for yourself. Here are a few simple systems to get you started.

Use Three-Ring Binders

A simple place to store paperwork you want available for use is the common three-ring binder. Plastic-tabbed index pages make it possible to divide items chronologically, alphabetically, or by subject matter. Using identical, solid-colored binders gives a neat and professional look. Color-coding the binders for visual identification works well, too, and sets a livelier mood. Try to break your materials down to fit into the two-inch size binders for easy handling with one hand. Be sure to label the spine of each binder for quick identification.

Ring binders can be used in the office for such items as copies of form letters, purchasing and shipping logs, file inventories, computer disk directories, or master copies of form documents. (HINT: Plastic sheet protectors on the latter will keep the masters in good photocopying shape.) Use three-ring binders for contact directories put out by the various unions, organizations, and corporations with which you deal (see Principle #4). Use binders for personal letters you want to save (copy or paste onto 81/2-x-11 sheets, or insert into plastic sheet protectors, if necessary). Use binders to store articles you've collected from newspapers and other sources. Again, tabbed dividers can be used to organize each binder further. I keep a binder for ideas for stories or other creative projects that occur to me.

If you have access to a transcriber and typewriter or word processor, using three-ring binders is a great way to keep a diary or journal. Carry a recorder with you and dictate ideas that occur to you, or reactions to daily events. Keep the recorder at your bedside for easy capture of your dreams (see Principle #9). Transcribe the tapes and file the pages in the binder. By getting everything down on tape while it's still a fresh experience, you'll probably find you have a more accurate, complete—and emotionally exciting—account of your life.

Use three-ring binders to hold your recipes. Plastic sheet protectors allow you to easily wipe off any spills that might occur while cooking. Actually, there are several simple ways to store recipes: a magnetic photo album; a Rolodex system using color-coded plastic covers to protect and identify categories; and the old-fashioned way of keeping index cards in a small file box. Each has pluses and minuses, so consider space and preference when selecting your method. The important thing is to find a uniform manner that works for you and use it consistently.

If you attend classes or seminars, use loose-leaf notebook paper in a ring binder to take notes, then hole-punch any handouts received and add them to the binder. Odd-sized handouts can be photocopied to the proper size or folded and filed either in the pockets on the front and back cover of many ring binders or in one of the three-hole pocket pages obtainable wherever office supplies are sold. Now, long after the class is completed, you will have a concise reference manual of the material.

Ring binders remove messy clutter from desks or table tops. They allow quick retrieval of information. Think over the permanent papers in your life and determine which can be better organized by this simple tool.

File for Easy Access

We've already mentioned how important it is to save receipts for tax purposes (see Principle #2). Corporations typically have elaborate systems for posting and filing such information. If bookkeeping is your area of responsibility, review the present system for possible simplification. Whether you use a ledger, budget book or computer to keep track of expenditures, you must still have an organized method for storing receipts.

Some people prefer using a file drawer or cabinet with labeled file folders. If you choose this method, invest in both hanging and manila file folders. This way, when you pull out the manila folder to look for information, the hanging folder will mark the spot so you can quickly find its place later. (HINT: If you get the pocket-style manila folders, small papers won't slip out the sides.)

In the home, your filing system will be less cumbersome than at the office. I use a very simple setup of five separate, pocket-type manila files.

* Bills to be paid
* Pending items (orders placed, refunds due, etc.)
* Flyers or catalogs I may want to order from
* Information I want to keep that is not conducive to ring binder storage
* Warranty information, service books and contracts, instruction booklets, and original purchase receipts on major appliances, equipment, furniture, etc.

The latter file is invaluable if, say, your VCR or oven goes on the fritz. Knowing exactly where to find all the information that you need to get the repairs done (hopefully free!) helps remove some of the stress from an already stressful situation.

In addition to these five pocket files, I have a large accordion file with about twenty dividers. I think mine originally had alphabetical tabs, but I made my own labels for each section: one for each deductible expense (as shown on Schedule C of the income tax form); one for income receipts (check stubs, etc.); one for nondeductible receipts (which I only keep one year); and one for bank statements and canceled checks.

Look over your filing system for ways to simplify it. Can large files be broken down into smaller, more precise topics? Would different, more descriptive categories work better? Are there any duplicate categories that can be combined or eliminated?

Let me give you an example. As art clerical for Target Stores advertising department (back in the days before computers), one of my duties was to pull previously created artwork to be reused in a current ad. When I began working for Target, old artwork was filed in thick files by generic item names-boys'shirts, ladies'dresses, etc.-and I would literally have to look at each piece on file and compare it with the picture on the flyer where it had been previously advertised. Not only was this very tedious, but publishing wrong artwork was an inherent problem of this system. By revamping the system to file the artwork by style number, not only was it virtually impossible to pull the wrong art, but it took seconds to go to a file labeled, for instance, Items 6800-6900, and pull out the art for Item 6825. Yes, it was a big job to make the change, but well worth the effort, believe me.

Another simple thing you can do to make referring back to files easier is to always file in date order, the most current papers to the front of the file. This puts the most recent items, which are generally the ones you need, right on top when the file is open in front of you.

Here is a word of caution about reorganizing filing systems at offices. One, do not do this when you first start a new job. Wait until you have a clear picture of how the files are used and why the current system is designed as it is. And two, be sure anyone who must access the files understands your new system. (HINT: Sometimes just straightening the papers and putting them into crisp, freshly labeled folders makes them seem more organized.)

The important thing to remember as you make your decision on a filing system is to select one that fits comfortably into your particular lifestyle and establish a habit of using it (see Principle #8).

Break Large Tasks into Small, Orderly Steps

Any major task is easier to accomplish if you break it into smaller segments. Say you want to clean the garage, attic, or storage room that currently looks like a twister hit it. The clutter eats at you, but you are too overwhelmed by the chore of organizing it to know where to start. If you can afford it, you can hire someone who specializes in organizing and cleaning to get you on top of things. The only problem with bringing in outside help is that you will hopefully be discarding a lot of the accumulation and only you can make the decision on which items to keep and which to let go. So why not do the task yourself and spend the money on a vacation? The suggestions below should help simplify the project.

Learn the first rule for large projects: Don't be afraid to make a mess. Start in one corner and pull everything out of the room—or at least into a pile in the middle of the floor. Then pick up one item at a time and do something with it. If it can be discarded, have a large trash bag handy and put it in there. If it is to be kept, decide where you want to store it and put it there. (HINT: When storing boxes of items, label the box on all sides so you can easily see what's in it.) If something can be recycled, start a bag or box for that. If you find one piece of paper to be filed, file it. If there are several papers to file, put them in a box to be sorted and filed later (a good task to do while watching television, see Principle #9).

Once one item is dealt with, proceed to the next. By focusing on one tiny piece of the chaos at a time, you'll be amazed when you suddenly realize the deed is done. Spread the task out over several days or weeks if you have to, accepting the work-in-progress mess for the eventual good of your household.

If your closet is jammed with clothes and you have nothing to wear, it's time to reorganize. Again, the first step is to pull everything out of the closet, or closets if your wardrobe has spilled over into several. Get four large boxes and label them: repair or revamp, use for rags, give to a friend, garage sale or charity. Now go through each item of clothing and try it on. Examine yourself in the mirror. Do you like the way it looks on you? Does it fit comfortably? Do you like how it makes you feel? Have you worn this article of clothing in the last six months? If you answer "no" to any one of these questions, put the item into one of the four boxes. If you

21

answer "yes" to all of the questions, straighten the article on the hanger and hang it back in the closet. (HINT: If you use more than one closet, put items you wear frequently in the most convenient one and less frequently worn items in the others; or set up the closets by seasons and rotate the items accordingly.)

Moving is another large task that can be simplified by breaking it into orderly steps. As you pack, label each box by room. As you unload, carry each box to its marked location. Situate your large items first (see Principle #2), then fill in with the small items, deciding where each will go and putting it there one item at a time.

Take a Fresh Look

Occasionally, a seemingly simple procedure suddenly becomes difficult. If you're getting bogged down in a task, take another look at it. Examine the project from all angles; maybe a completely different approach from the one you are using will work better. Don't be afraid to start over.

Sometimes the system you're using is fine, but the task still seems too difficult to complete. For instance, if you're trying to balance your checkbook or financial report, or to organize a thesis or manuscript, and you become hopelessly confused, forget everything you've just done and start over. I rewrote this book several times in completely different ways before I finally felt that it looked and said what I wanted it to say.

Use lists to get you back on track (see Principle #2). Somehow, boiling problems down into numbered notes makes them seem less formidable. If you're confused about where you are and where you're going on a project, take a break. Put your feet up and have a cup of tea. With pen and paper in hand, imagine completing the task, step-by-step, writing each step down in a numbered list as if you are writing an instruction booklet or recipe even a child could follow. Once you get the list made, just do each numbered item in order until you are done.

Speaking of children, if all else fails, look at the daunting task or system from a child's point of view. Maybe even consult one about your problem. Children have a knack of looking at things in the simplest possible terms. It's a talent we adults seem to forget we have. Maybe it's time to reacquaint ourselves with the child inside.

Description of my Inner Child:

_____

_____

_____

_____

_____

_____

_____

_____

_____

_____

It is easy
to maintain a situation
while it is still secure;
It is easy to deal with a situation
before symptoms develop;
It is easy to break a thing
when it is yet brittle;
It is easy to dissolve a thing
when it is yet minute.
Deal with a thing
while it is still nothing;
Keep a thing in order
before disorder sets in.

"Efficiency that leads to success is developed through concentration and meditation."

Paramahansa
Yogananda

Principle Four:
Write Things Down

The written record frees our brains of distractions that hamper our efficiency. Just as a computer takes longer to operate on a large file than on a small one, so your brain will work more slowly if it is cluttered with thoughts and ideas unrelated to the task at hand. The best way to remove such clutter from the working memory of your brain is to write things down. Carry a small notebook or a tape recorder with you at all times and jot down any intruding idea of value. Once you know these thoughts are preserved for when you want them, you can forget about them for the time being and concentrate on your current project.

Life Goals

Writing down our goals is something most of us would go to the dentist to avoid doing. But it is important because when you write something down you give it energy. That alone helps you reach your goal. The good news is that this is really an ongoing process that can be easily accomplished with a few basic tools and tips.

Using the ideal life you imagined and wrote down at the beginning of this book, now list every practical step you can take to achieve that ideal. For example, if you want to be a writer, your list might include the following: take a creative writing class or attend writers' seminars; read all the books you can find in the genre in which you are interested in writing;

buy a computer; join a group or online chat room for writers; study the annual Writer's Market reference book; start a savings account; start a three-ring binder of story ideas.

If you want to own a chain of hotels, your list might include these tasks: get a job in the hotel industry, even if entry-level; enroll in hotel management classes at the local college; apply for management training at a hotel; interview a successful president of a major hotel chain (by letter if necessary), asking for advice or mentoring; read biographies of successful businesspeople; scout locations to build your first hotel; establish a good credit rating and save, save, save.

As you can see by these two examples, there are things you can begin to do at any age, under any circumstances, to reach your goals. As you proceed, your list will probably grow. That's okay. Writing everything down gives you a list of concrete steps to make your dream come true. Now you simply begin to schedule the completion of each step, one per month—or even year—if that's all your current situation allows. It is the process of working toward your goals that is the most exciting. If you don't believe that, take the first step, even if small, and observe the thrill of hope it brings.

Monthly Goals

There are many planning/appointment calendars on the market. Browse through the display racks in your local stores to find the one that best fits your needs. I use a thin book with one double-page per month because it is lightweight and easy to carry in my purse, but you should get the book that takes the least amount of time and effort for you to maintain. If it becomes too complicated, you won't use it.

At the beginning of each year, under the appropriate days in this calendar book, enter every one of your known obligations for the year. For example, on the first Tuesday of each month, note that you attend the monthly meeting of Rabble-Rousers Anonymous. On every other Monday, note that you drive the carpool. Enter the rent and other payments on the date they're due each month. (HINT: If you plan to mail the payment, enter it under the date it must be mailed in order to arrive by the actual due date.) Enter such things as: car insurance due on January 30 and July 30; homeowner's or renter's insurance due on March 14; income tax due on April 15; registration and driver's license renewal dates. If you're planning your vacation around a particular event or at a particular time, enter that.

Carry this book with you and enter all firm obligations when you make the commitment: take the dog to the vet; schedule a pay raise review with your boss; go to brunch and a movie matinee with a friend; make a presentation to a new client; enroll in extension classes at the local college. For the latter, write the class dates and times in their appropriate spots. Now you are ready to prepare your Things-to-Do Diary.

Things-to-Do Diary

I use a 6-x-9-inch spiral-bound notebook for my daily tasks, a page for each day. It's easy to carry in my briefcase, has just the right amount of room on each page, and by keeping it intact, I have an excellent record of exactly when I did one thing or another. Depending on how many different things you have to do each day, you may want to use a larger spiral-bound notebook, or a smaller one. Whichever you select, this notebook will be the notepad for your life. Here's how it works.

First write the day of the week and date at the top of each page, one per day, working a month ahead at a time. (HINT: Use pencil to make it easier and neater to change things as necessary.) Once each page is labeled, go through the monthly appointment book (above) and transfer the upcoming month's obligations to the corresponding notebook page.

Next look at your list of steps toward your ideal life (above). Enter at least one step sometime throughout the month, on a day it can conceivably be accomplished. A more complicated step can be broken down over several days if necessary. Naturally, scheduling more than one step per month will move you more quickly toward your goal. For example, to start an at-home business, you might one day schedule to brainstorm alone or with others about a name for the business; another day call the courthouse for information on obtaining a business license; another day go apply for the license; another day visit a business similar to the one you plan and observe how they operate. Whatever your case may be, making a written commitment to complete the steps necessary to achieve your dream will make it a reality.

Enter new obligations as they arise throughout the month. For instance, when I drop film off for developing, I make a note to pick up the pictures on the day they will be ready. I do the same thing with picking up dry cleaning, returning a library book or videos. If the follow-up date falls into the next month, you can enter it in your monthly calendar book for now, or date your spiral pages even further ahead. Enter important calls to be made. (HINT: Look up and enter the phone number in the book at the same time. It is way too easy to procrastinate making calls if you have to stop and look up the number during the day.) Enter plays, movies or concerts you want to see, and television programs you want to watch or record. And don't forget family time!

Once you have written down everything you need and want to do, both personally and professionally, you can prioritize your day each morning as you have your morning coffee. Don't get hung up in a 1-2-3 process. Instead sort into four categories:

   * *Priority A: I have to do this as soon as possible.*
   * *Priority B: I should do this before the end of the day.*
   * *Priority C: I would feel good if I got these things done today.*
   * *Priority X: I want to complete this by the end of the month. If I have time to get to it today, great. If not, I won't hate myself.*

Now, as you go about your day, jot down notes on anything you come across during your day that might be helpful to remember: a phone number or address received; an idea to follow up on at a later date. I doodle notes during phone conversations to refresh my memory later on what was discussed and carry the notebook to meetings to jot down details settled on during the discussions. If your schedule is complex and takes up the whole page, make these notes on the back side of the previous day's page so that when the notebook is opened flat, your notes will be on the left sheet, your things-to-do on the right. As you accomplish each listed task, check it off. At the end of the day, if something did not get done, don't beat yourself up about it, just move it to the next day.

Of all the suggestions I make in this book, keeping this notebook has proven to be the most useful to everyone I have mentioned it to, for many reasons. It is invaluable to show if and when something was done. If you consistently keep such a record, even the IRS will generally accept it as backup for a deductible expense. I have even used mine in court to win a case against a landlord who was trying to keep my security deposit.

The notebook comes in handy when corresponding with friends. You can look up the last time you wrote and then flip forward to see what news or activities can be shared in a new letter. This is especially helpful if you write to many people and can't always remember who you told what to and don't want to appear senile by repeating yourself.

The notebook makes excellent backup for preparing status reports on projects or asking for a raise. You can be very specific about ways you have been of benefit to the company by flipping through the pages since your last raise. It can also be a lifesaver to show you've taken care of something, or in locating an important phone number that your boss has misplaced.

There are now many incredible computer software programs and electronic organizers to aid in planning your time as well. If your schedule is complicated, this type of system may be essential. On the other hand, such programs may take more time to use than they save, especially if your schedule is simple. Another advantage of the handwritten record, of course, is that, unless you have a laptop computer, the notebook is at your fingertips at all times.

Again, only you can decide what works for you. Whatever method you choose—even if it's using a lone piece of scratch paper—get these daily tasks written down. It's the best way to get them completed efficiently, and a wonderful way to reinforce your feelings of accomplishment.

Tickler Files

Keeping reminder notes in a tickler file is an important aid to our often faulty human memory. If you have only a few items outstanding, using the manila pocket files suggested in Principle #3 (for pending items, bills to be paid, etc.) may be enough.

A more complex tickler file is broken down by day and month and holds all paperwork or notes on pending items (i.e., letters that need follow-up, the actual bills to be paid, notes on tasks you need to accomplish by a certain date). A Globe-Weis Everyday file works well for this. Smead also makes a similar one. Get the kind that is indexed from 1-to-31 in the front and January-to-December in the back. Indexed accordion files work, too, although they are too bulky for my taste and small papers sometimes slip under the dividers.

Put shoe repair, dry cleaning, film developing, or similar tickets under the date to be picked up. Put your concert or theater tickets under the day of the show. Any paperwork you'll need to accomplish the items in your Things-to-Do Diary should be in the tickler file. Check the tickler file and pull paperwork each morning as you organize your day.

Tickler files, in conjunction with Things-to-Do Diaries, prevent important tasks from slipping through the cracks.

Personal Dictionaries

Every business comes with its own professional jargon. If you are new to the field, it is very helpful to enter any unfamiliar words and their definitions into a notebook as you encounter them. If you have to verify the spelling of a frequently used word, add it to the notebook as well. Keep your list in a ring binder, using alphabetically tabbed sections for easy referral.

Computers make this task even easier. Use the table format of your word-processing program or any database program and set up three columns: one for the word, one for the pronunciation, and one for the definition. You can then alphabetize these at the push of a button and also easily find the word you need by using the software's search feature.

This personal dictionary is also an effective tool for increasing your vocabulary and knowledge base. Have you ever heard a new word or name, wondered at the meaning, and then within a short period of time heard it again? This has happened to me more times than I can say. For example, I once heard the word *concomitant*. I was unfamiliar with it, so I looked up the correct spelling, pronunciation and definition and entered it in my personal dictionary. Within a month I had encountered the word in a conversation with a stranger, in a magazine article, and in a report I was transcribing. Each time I had a ready reference and the word became part of my vocabulary. The simple act of writing down the unfamiliar word and definition in your personal dictionary generally gives it more value to you and thereby helps you remember it—or if not, you'll be able to find it quickly. By the way, *concomitant* means happening at the same time or accompanying each other.

Along this same line, if you have a tendency to confuse certain words, make a note to yourself on brightly colored paper and tack it up where you can easily see it. For example, *its* is the possessive pronoun, *it's* is the contraction for *it is*. If you're like most people who continually mix these words up, a Post-it note beside your computer will remind you to search each document you type to be sure you've caught the typo that your spelling program won't catch.

Memos and Letters

In the business world, written correspondence is essential for organized operation. Memos, for example, take less time than meetings, provide a written record of communications, allow for more clarity of thoughts being transmitted, and give the responder time to formulate a suitable reply.

Memos and letters should be brief and easy-to-read. Break them into short, informal paragraphs or bulleted lists. State the facts clearly. Present pros and cons, wording everything positively. Conclude with a one-sentence summary and your recommended action.

Does the thought of putting words on paper terrify you? Here's where your imagination comes in again (see Principle #1). Visualize yourself in a conversation with the person to whom you are writing. Now simply transfer your portion of the conversation onto paper. Visualize the other person's reactions to your communication and answer any questions they might raise or counter any doubts or opposition they might express. If you are writing to more than one person, focus on the one with whom you are most comfortable. Letters and memos will be a snap.

Think of it this way: When writing, you are merely talking on paper. If your point is easily grasped and clearly understood, your memo or letter has achieved its purpose.

Logs

Logs are important in many areas and are easy to set up. Use three-ring binders and either loose-leaf notebook paper divided into hand-ruled columns; accountants' columnar pads with the applicable number of columns; or a custom master form created on your typewriter/word processor and photocopied. There are several good programs that are easy to use for computerized logs. Excel is my favorite, but again, select the one with which you are most comfortable. You may, in fact, have several logs and create a different type of form for each.

If you send bills to an outside accounting firm for payment, use a trusty ring binder to record invoices sent over, including the supplier's name and the amount of the invoice. This provides an easy record to check if there's a problem with payment or a question on an account status and saves paying high hourly rates to have the CPA look up the information for you.

By logging completed tasks on an ongoing projects log, you have a quick reference on the status of the project. If you're a writer, set up a log for your royalty payments to see at a glance how much you have earned from each book or music project and, as happened at Steve Allen's office, to catch errors in reporting these.

To keep track of where various documents can be found on your computer, put the printed directories in a ring binder. Some firms set up a standard file numbering system for computer files, with all documents logged on a form that shows file number, date, topic, and disk or directory information.

Most major corporations log incoming mail of importance. It's a good idea for even small firms. By including a column for date of response, you will be able to quickly spot which items have not yet been attended to.

I like to create a footer on each computer document, in an 8-pt. font, which gives the file and path name, and the date of last update, if that information is helpful. If your employer prefers not to have the notation on the document itself, write the information in pencil on the backside of your file copy. This one step can save hours of time searching disks and directories for a file you must revise or want to reuse six months later.

But logs can be even simpler. I have a friend, Sue, who has dozens of books and videotapes she is constantly lending to others. She has a very simple system for keeping track of what's out where: a plain piece of paper tacked on the wall. On it, she writes the person's name and items taken (which are crossed off when the items are returned). I lost many books through loan-outs that were never returned before I adopted this one simple procedure.

Index cards and a file box can also work for logs. This is how I keep track of my writing submissions. When I am ready to pitch a project, I make up a five-by-eight-inch index card with the title across the top and then eight columns labeled as follows: submission date, to whom, follow-up date, date accepted, amount to be paid, date payment due, date payment received, and date rejected. This shows the status of the project at a glance and avoids recontacting a publisher who may have already passed on the work. Another advantage is that if I list several potential buyers when I first begin submitting a piece, if one returns it I can quickly mail it out to the next on the list to soothe the rejection blues. This system also works for submitting anything for sale—photographs, craft items, whatever. While relevant paperwork will be filed by project name in a file cabinet, the simple card system gives all the information needed at a glance.

Address Files

To maintain organized address files, you should purchase a good address book, Rolodex-type system, electronic organizer, or a combination of these. I have a preprinted, loose-leaf address book for my personal numbers, a Rolodex for my business, and a large ring binder for organizational directories and specialized address lists. In the latter category, for instance, I have writer, agent, and producer lists put out by the applicable unions, which are filed in tabbed sections. Most of these are free, or can be purchased for a nominal cost.

If you are given many business cards in your line of work, business-card wallets or file boxes are an inexpensive way to organize them for easy reference. One word of caution about electronic organizers: Don't depend on them. My son recently discovered this the hard way when his organizer crashed and he had no written record of any of the numbers in it. Sometimes the old-fashioned way is still the best way.

If you keep business cards, write the product or service at the top of the card. In many cases it is faster to access the card if it is filed by this information rather than the company name.

Whatever system you select for your addresses and phone numbers, the important step, for maximum efficiency, is to enter contact information into it as soon as possible after you receive it. If you lose that name and number it will do you no good. (HINT: Enter information in pencil to keep such records neatly up-to-date, especially in our mobile society.)

Alphabetizing the names is so automatic it hardly seems worth mentioning, but I actually know people who will enter a name at the first open space they find and then look through their entire book every time they want to make a call. If this is you, get a new book and start over now.

If you use Rolodex cards, typing them makes them neater and easier to use. There are cards especially designed for use with your computer printer at most office supply stores, or you can use the plain Avery-type labels for printers. The latter method has the economical and ecological advantage of reusing the Rolodex cards by sticking a new label over the old one when information changes.

Each address entry should contain as much of the following information as is available: company name, complete address, phone numbers including extension number, fax number, e-mail address, contact names, product or service, and date the card was set up or updated. The latter is helpful in determining if information on a seldom-used card should be checked for validity before using. For business contacts, it's a good idea to include a home number, if possible, especially if time zones are a factor. Since so many of today's companies are answered by an automated menu, note with the phone number the menu selections to get you to the departments with whom you generally deal. With this information, you can just punch on through and not listen to the web of choices that waste your time and leave you dazed and confused.

Cross-referencing a Rolodex is a definite time saver. File a card under the company name and the contact person's name. Although you can put "see so-and-so" on one of the cards, why flip to two cards to get the information? The few extra seconds you spend entering all relevant data on both cards can save hours over the course of your working life.

Another important cross-reference card is the product or service card. You know that Joe Blow is the plumber, but if the toilet's overflowing and you're not available, the person who must handle the emergency will appreciate being able to flip to "plumber" for help in a hurry.

As a matter of fact, it's also helpful to have a one-page master list of shops that provide that general type of service—plumbers, electricians, painters, locksmiths, air conditioning specialists, burglar alarm installers, equipment servicemen, etc. Indicate if there is a maintenance agreement and any relevant account numbers or codes.

Type the name under which the card is to be filed in capital letters at the top left corner of the card: RIMSHOT, RAY. The MULBERRY CONNECTION. ELECTRICIAN. (HINT: On the duplicate, cross-reference cards, be sure your top, capitalized line shows how it is filed. For example, Joe Blow at Zanzabar Company would have one card headed ZANZABAR COMPANY and one headed BLOW, JOE.) This makes it easier to spot the card you need and to replace the card alphabetically when you are finished with it. You can also purchase brightly colored plastic covers that fit Rolodex cards and make for quick locating of those cards referred to frequently. (HINT: When removing a Rolodex card for use, put a small Post-it note or paper clip on the card immediately after it for quick replacement in the proper order.)

Most large organizations print corporate phone directories, organized by department, with an index by employee name. Ask for a copy of this directory from each corporation you deal with frequently, and be sure you're on the list for updates. By having the appropriate name and direct number available, you avoid wasting time being transferred from department to department or waiting for a response to a letter that must be re-routed to the person who can answer it. Another bonus of corporate directories is that they quickly advise you of the proper spelling of names. This saves you the time and expense of calling for that information. Using correct spellings of names—and correct titles—is just one way to let others know you value them. And feeling valued elicits cooperation. If you frequently do business in cities other than your own, obtain phone directories for those cities. You can also find directories for most major cities at your local library or online.

If you want to computerize your contact information, there are many good software programs to make this easy. Action Planner is one. This program actually allows you to print a phone book with yellow pages. Now that's convenience. Again, however, consider input and use time. Manual systems are sometimes more practical.

If an address or phone number changes, enter the new information as soon as it is received. If you wait, these changes tend to pile up and entering them becomes a chore you avoid. Meanwhile, you waste time looking for information that has not yet been entered in its proper place, or worse, send a letter off to the wrong destination only to have it returned, costing you not only time but money.

Personal Journals

If you are not keeping a personal journal, you are missing out on what more and more people are touting as the most valuable tool available for living a blissful life. Whether you use a small, locked diary, a composition or spiral-bound notebook, a word processing program or a three-ring binder system, I beg you to try writing in a journal every day for the next twenty-one days. Journals help you discover who you really are beneath all the frustrations and triumphs and roles you play in everyday life. They help you be the master of your emotions and achieve your destiny. They help you collect your thoughts and preserve your inspirations. They help you document your past so you don't repeat mistakes or place too much importance on "the small stuff." A journal is your direct connection to your divinity. Of all the harmonious habits we can cultivate (see Principle #8), I sincerely believe journaling is the most important for our growth as spiritual beings. The positive effect of journaling in my life is a book in itself.

There are many excellent books on the market about keeping journals. Some advocate writing two or three pages every day. Some say to set a timer for as little as fifteen minutes of time and then write as quickly as you can about whatever pops into your head. Some tout a combination of these and other techniques. Some say to write when you first get up; some when you retire for the evening. Whatever way works for you, the time spent recapping the old day and anticipating the new will change your life.

You don't have to be a writer to keep a journal. You don't have to be witty or wise. The pages are for you and you alone—to serve as a dumping ground for the negatives in your life and a staging area for the positives. Please, please try it.

There are many other ways a written record can better organize your day, free the clutter from your brain, and back up your fallible memory. Explore areas in your life where writing things down will pay big dividends in efficiency.

The Way
never acts
Yet
Nothing
is left
undone

*Your ability
to do a job
is directly
proportional
to your desire
to do it.*

Principle Five:
Use assembly line principles

There is a reason why factories use assembly-line principles: They are the most efficient way to get a routine job accomplished. Assembly lines recognize and incorporate two important traits of the human brain. The first is that our brains can only effectively concentrate on one thing at a time. Secondly, if the brain sends out the same signal for action more than a few times in a row, it remembers, and will begin to accomplish the task automatically—and thus faster.

Anything that is done more than once a week should have some kind of system, form, or form letter. Assembly-line principles can be used to streamline every area of our lives. Below are a few specific examples.

Attending to Incoming Mail

If your job includes processing incoming mail, first, pull out any mail you do not open and start a pile or folder for the recipient. Next, turn the remaining envelopes over and slit them open. Now go back and pull out the papers, date-stamp them, and sort them for distribution. Unless your company is large enough for everyone to have a mailbox, use a manila file folder for each person or department, or just put the letters into individual piles. (HINT: If you use folders, make up a couple for each person and ask them to return them so you can rotate their use.) The important thing here, in order to be organized, is to put the same person's pile or folder in the same position on your desk or countertop every time you sort the mail, with the person who gets the most mail the closest. After only a couple of days, your hand will automatically move toward that spot with that person's mail, making the sorting more automatic, and thus more efficient.

If you receive a lot of mail, or you're responsible for organizing your boss's mail, use manila file folders, typing labels for the tabs or labeling the front of the folder with a magic marker, perhaps color-coding it— red for urgent, green for invoices to be approved, etc. Categories can include the following:

Priority 1 (urgent; attend to today)

Priority 2 or No Rush (letters that aren't urgent; ongoing personal correspondence)

FYI (for your information; no response necessary)

Invoices to be approved

Catalogs and sales brochures

Newsletters and other reading materials

Before you add the new mail each day, take the folders from your boss's desk and go through any papers that have not been attended to. Should any be moved from Priority 2 to Priority 1, for instance? Are the most important items on top? Highlight or underline the main information in each letter so that your employer will be able to see all pertinent information at a glance. If a letter refers to previous correspondence, clip that to the new item. If a form letter is applicable, attach a copy for appropriate revisions. Or prepare a draft response for your boss's approval. If you answer any mail for your boss, put the original letter and a copy of your reply into the FYI file to keep hir informed. Place all papers into the proper folders with the most important (or oldest) correspondence on top.

This same system, slightly modified, can be applied to the paperwork on your own desk, or papers at home. Folders keep things neat, and neatness always increases efficiency.

Don't waste time on junk mail. In fact, the ecological alternative is to get your name removed from junk mail lists. To do this, notify one of the companies you can find by searching the Internet by keywords "stop junk mail." Or you can tear the label off unwanted mail and return it with a brief note to the sender, asking to be removed from future mailings. You can also specify, when buying from mail-order catalogs, that the company not put your name on any mailing lists to begin with.

Sending Greeting Cards

While it's a good idea to keep a box of assorted greeting cards on hand for unexpected occasions that pop up, it's nice to select a greeting especially for the individual to whom it is being given. Here's how an assembly-line system can keep your greeting card buying and sending more organized.

Get a small diary or calendar book that is not year-specific. Enter birthdays, anniversaries and other important greeting card days into the book under the appropriate day. After the name, enter the year of birth or the wedding in parentheses. When there are new births and marriages, add these immediately upon receiving the announcement.

At the end of each month, flip through the next month's diary pages and list those to whom you will send cards. Take the list to your favorite card shop and-Voila!-in just slightly more time than it takes to buy one card, you will have all your cards for the month.

If you receive an invitation for a special one-time-only event that requires a card or gift, put the invitation with the diary, unless it's in the current month and your cards are already prepared. In that case, put the invitation in your tickler file and add it to your Things-To-Do Diary. If a card that would be perfect for someone not on your list catches your eye, go ahead and buy it, storing it with your Things-To-Do Diary until it is needed. (Have you ever noticed how you can never find those perfect cards again if you wait to purchase them?)

I make all my cards on the computer, using a couple of different software programs now available, but I still set aside one day at the end of each month to make all the cards for the following month and get them ready to mail (see below).

Once you have your cards, immediately address them. Calculate the mail date (if applicable) and pencil it in a bottom corner of the envelope. If the card is to be hand-delivered, write the date of the event. Sign the card, adding a small personal note. Even though this card may say everything you want to say exactly how you want to say it, your own personal note adds a special touch. Only those cards in which you want to enclose a last-minute letter should be left open. The rest are sealed; all are stamped.

Make notes to mail the cards under the appropriate days in your Things-To-Do Diary and file the envelopes under the corresponding days in your tickler file (see Principle #4). The pencil notation can then be erased.

Christmas/Hanukkah cards are handled a bit differently but just as easily. If you use boxed cards, try to find some you like during the after-Christmas sales and buy them for the following year. Otherwise, buy them in the fall, in an otherwise slow card month. Any individual cards you send for the holidays can be purchased with your regular November or December cards. Sometime between when you buy them and December 15, schedule a time to sit down and address the cards. Make yourself comfortable, put the blank envelopes to your left and, taking one at a time, address the envelope and place it in one of two piles to the right—those that will get a short note on the card and those that will get a longer letter. Even though you may have a long holiday mailing list, and some are going to business acquaintances or your next door neighbor whom you talk to every day, even one line of a personal greeting will make the card more special. Next sign all the cards in the note stack, jotting the message on the card as you sign. Insert the card in the envelope and seal.

Although many people hate holiday form letters, they make sound sense from an organized person's point of view. Fortunately, with word processors, you can personalize such letters. Enter the basic news you want to share, then edit in recipient-specific comments and questions. Once the first letter is printed, retain the general news of the letter, change the personal paragraphs to fit the next recipient, and so on. They'll never know it's a form letter. Again, finish in assembly-line style—signing, folding, stuffing, sealing and stamping the items in short order.

Unless you live alone, it's a fun idea to include the family in this project. Let one person sign the cards; another address the envelope; another stuff and seal; and another stamp (naturally split or combine these duties to accommodate the number of members in your family). Add a little holiday music, some hot chocolate, lively family reminiscences of the person to whom the card is going, and it becomes a much-anticipated yearly event.

If you don't have a word processor, or you don't want to use a form letter, even if it is personalized, split up the letter writing with other members of the family, letting each recap the year in hir own words (comparing the versions can be very interesting and enlightening). Another alternative is to let each person tell about hir own activities of the year and enclose the separate accounts as one letter. Whatever way works best in your family, fusing the process with holiday cheer will make it an event not a chore. If you send out cards on other holidays, just include these in the birthday-card process.

Of course, there is now a wonderful alternative to the whole holiday greeting business. Many worthwhile charity organizations now offer a holiday gift/greeting system. You make a donation, sending a list of names and addresses to whom you want greetings sent. The organization does all the work of sending the cards that greet your friends and let them know a donation has been made in their honor. Not only does this save you an incredible amount of time, but it truly reflects the spirit of the season. Check with your favorite charity about this truly caring alternative to the sadly commercialized holiday-card-sending ritual.

Reading the Newspaper

Reading the newspaper can be one of the most time-consuming activities you perform on a regular basis. It is an excellent place to use assembly-line principles. First of all, unless in-depth knowledge of late-breaking news is vital to your goals (i.e., you must know the stock reports each morning), there is no reason for busy people to buy a daily paper. A short time listening to the radio or TV news while dressing, doing chores, or driving to work or the kids to school can keep you abreast of the outside world throughout the week. With so many of us on the Internet today, we can also keep abreast of late-breaking information by this manner, checking out the details of only those stories that we must know more about.

Sunday papers, however, pay for themselves if you're a coupon-clipper, and they provide recaps of the weekly stories to keep you informed. Before you sit down with the newspaper, grab the scissors, and a cup of coffee, if you like. Now you are ready to open the paper and separate it into sections. Discard those sections you have no interest in. For instance, I never read the sport pages unless there are play-offs going on. I don't read the want ads unless I am job or house hunting, curious about salaries, or wanting to buy something. However, occasionally I glance through the personal columns for story ideas.

Unless you're in the market for something specific, reading the slick advertising sections only tempts you to spend money on something you probably don't need. An exception would be if you are looking for a specific, big-ticket item and want to skim the flyers for sale prices.

Scan the coupon pages and cut out those items you would normally buy or you've been thinking about trying. Put the rest in your discard pile. If you are currently throwing coupons away, consider this: You are throwing away money. With so many markets doubling certain coupons, the savings you can rack up with coupons is incredible. The other day, I spent $9.95 for groceries that would have cost me $14.00. If you follow the procedure outlined under Principle #2, you will soon wonder why you ever considered this more hassle than what is saved.

Once you have dealt with the unnecessary sections, arrange the others in the order you will read them. It's a good idea to put the ones that can be read most quickly on top. By putting the more time-consuming sections toward the end, you'll be less likely to dawdle over them.

Skim the headlines and then focus on only those items that interest you. Most newspapers provide convenient summary sections that will keep you well-enough informed on most news. Longer articles or ones you want to digest fully can be cut out and read during a future waiting period (see Principle #9).

Don't neglect the comics. They offer a chuckle and sometimes interesting insights. Consider them ambrosia for your soul.

I enjoy the crossword puzzles, but unless I'm in a mood to kick back for the day, I cut these out and carry them in a folder in my briefcase to do during waiting periods. Be sure to indulge in whatever section is your favorite.

Place each section on the discard pile as you finish reading it, and don't forget to recycle. (HINT: If other members of your family also read the Sunday paper, get up early to be able to have the paper to yourself or wait until later in the day when they've gone on to other things.)

Balancing Your Checkbook

Many people don't balance their checkbook on a monthly basis because it seems like too much trouble or they have never been taught how to do it. But it is important for catching bank errors (yes, they do make mistakes!), as well as your own. And using the assembly-line principle makes it a breeze.

Many banks now shred canceled checks and send you small copies or list cleared checks in check number order. If you still get your canceled checks, your first step in balancing your checkbook is to put them in check number order. If you write only a few checks, this is easy to do by fanning and shuffling them into order like you do playing cards.

If you have a lot of canceled checks, however, it's usually easiest to sort them first into piles of ten, all the 1570s together, 1580s, 1620s, whatever. By laying the piles out in ascending numerical order in front of you, once you have the first check down for each group, you can quickly deal the remaining checks onto their respective piles. You'll find that after a few checks are down, your hand will automatically go to the correct pile, without you even having to look. Once all the checks are in piles, simply shuffle each pile of ten into order by fanning them in your hand.

Now go through your checkbook register and put a checkmark by each check that has cleared. (HINT: There is a little box next to each entry on your check register for this.) As you mark off each check, compare what is entered in your check register against what the bank has coded at the bottom of the check. If the amount is different, but what you made your check out for and what you recorded in your checkbook matches, the bank has made an error. Make a note and call them to correct it. If it's your mistake, write in the correction at the end of your register and add or subtract it from your checkbook balance. If the check, the bank and your check register all agree, breeze on.

Now go through your statement, checking off teller machine transactions, automatic payments, or direct deposits in both your checkbook register and on the bank statement. If you haven't written an item into your checkbook, do so now and update your check register balance. Enter any bank service charges into your checkbook register, put a checkmark beside them, and update your ending balance. If everything listed in your check register page has cleared the bank and is therefore checked off, write the word "all" on the bottom of that page. This lets you know you don't have to waste time looking through the page when listing outstanding items.

Now flip through your checkbook, stopping at any page that doesn't have "all" written at the bottom. List the outstanding checks or deposits (those you haven't checked off) on the reconciliation form provided on the back of the bank statement.

Enter the ending balance shown on the bank statement on the reconciliation form. Add the outstanding deposits you have listed, and subtract the outstanding checks. If that number doesn't match the ending balance of your checkbook register, your account is out of balance.

If this is the case, immediately double-check all your checkmarks and arithmetic to be sure you didn't miss anything. This includes adding and subtracting all checkbook entries since you last balanced it. Also double-check to be sure you're using the correct bank balance, the ending balance. (HINT: If the amount you are off is divisible by nine, you may have transposed a number. Look for where you might have entered or added $79.00, for instance, instead of $97.00, or twenty-one cents instead of twelve.)

If you simply cannot find the error, you can do one of two things: you can go to the bank customer service department, taking all the statements you've received from the bank since the last time you were in balance, and have them help you reconcile the account; or you can accept the bank's balance as correct and change your checkbook balance to match. This is called force-balancing and should be avoided if at all possible.

Another thing that sometimes works is to set the project aside and go back to it later, starting completely over and using a different colored pen or a dot instead of a checkmark to identify cleared items. Sometimes the fresh look at the problem is all you need to quickly find your mistake (see Principle #3). If you were in balance the previous month, but you absolutely can't find the discrepancy this time, make a note of it and let it ride until your next statement. It generally works itself out. If it doesn't, you may have to go to the bank and get it resolved—unless the fresh look at the out-of-balance reconciliation reveals your error.

Once in balance, draw a pencil line across your checkbook under the last listed balance and write "OK" and the date. By doing this, if you don't balance the next month, you will know that the mistake has to be between this line and the latest entry in your register. If there is a bank error to be corrected, call the bank, making a note of the date and person spoken to in your checkbook so that you can check the following month's statement to be sure the bank made the correction.

You are now done. Return the checks and statement to the mailing envelope (or a file, if that's how you store them), writing on the front of the envelope the date and if the statement is in balance, or how much it is off and why.

Be sure to keep a running checkbook balance. It's not necessary to calculate the new balance each time you write a check, but every few days you should fill in the balances, at least at the top and the bottom of each register page. (HINT: If you enter the balances in pencil, corrections can be made neatly, and the neater your checkbook, the more apt you'll be to keep it in balance.)

Organizing Cabinets and Drawers

Have you ever noticed that you can walk into almost any kitchen in the world and easily locate the silverware drawer, a glass in the cupboard, the dish soap, etc.? Or that you can go into an office and know which drawer holds the pencils, which the backup office supplies, which the daily files?

This is because most of us instinctively use assembly-line principles when organizing our workspaces in order to streamline our motions. We put our wastebaskets close to where we make the most trash. We put our cooking utensils and spices close to the stove or work counter; our pens, pencils and stationary are kept in easy reach.

If your work areas are not arranged this way, you are losing efficiency in wasted motions. To correct this, visualize yourself in your workspace. Imagine wanting to use each item stored there and watch where you reach for it with the least amount of movement and effort. That is where the item should be kept.

Another trick I have for saving time is to keep my pens, pencils and scissors on the top of my desk in a decorative holder. At home, I have coffee mugs or fancy jars filled with pens, pencils, scissors, a ruler, letter opener, etc. in each room, close to where I use them. Incidentally, I also keep a box of Kleenex and a wastebasket in each room. The time and energy this simple practice saves me is readily evident.

Cleaning the House

No one wants to spend any more time than they have to on this necessary chore. The easiest way to clean a house is to take a room a day, rotating them in the same sequence so that each room gets cleaned at a regular interval. This system keeps the task from becoming a big deal. Once in awhile, however, like when a houseguest is scheduled, you will want to do a broad sweep of the house.

Before you start, put on some music. My favorite for this is reggae because the beat sets an efficient, stress-free tempo—but any music that puts you in an energetic mood works.

Begin by cruising through the house and straightening the disarray. Discard items no longer needed, put things away that have been left out. If there are furniture throws, bed sheets or the like that have to be laundered, pull them off and start them now. Next, pick up the rugs throughout the house, take them outside for shaking, and then leave them outside to air out and to be out of your way until the room is cleaned.

Now go through the house with glass cleaner, then with furniture polish. Straighten knickknacks and books as you dust them off. If you prefer to do everything in one room at a time, load your cleaners and rags into a pail for easy carting from room to room.

The bathroom appliances get the next attention; then the kitchen's. If you have a refrigerator that needs defrosting, turn it off the night before or earlier in the day so that it will be ready to be wiped down when you get to this stage of cleaning. Fortunately, most refrigerators are now frost-free.

Next wash the floors. (HINT: A one-step product saves time by washing and waxing concomitantly.) Be sure to plan ahead so you don't trap yourself where you don't want to be. If you can, it also works well to wash floors before you go to bed so they can dry overnight. (HINT: Set wastebaskets on counters, move chairs to another room. The fewer things left on the floor, the faster and easier it will be to wash it.) While the floors are drying, attack the carpets, drapes, blinds, etc. with the vacuum.

Lay the rugs back on the floor, put the laundered sheets and throws in their place, and you're done.

Now, light a scented candle, pour yourself a beverage, and sit back and admire your accomplishment for fifteen minutes. You deserve the break!

Naturally, the order of doing things given here, like everything else offered, is just a suggestion. The important thing is to clean regularly. It will do wonders for your mood. And if you can wheedle or pay the kids to do it. . . .

Before I leave this section, I simply must throw in a couple of helpful hints, just because I am a helpful-hint addict.

Baking soda is a great cleaner, especially to keep refrigerators sweet smelling. Pour some down the drain to keep it fresh, too, and add a vinegar "chaser" for a homemade drain-clearer. Baking soda also works great on your car and, well, just about everything.

Hydrogen peroxide is also a cheap alternative cleaner. You can clean almost any spot from white carpets, upholstery, and clothes in a snap with this wonderful liquid. Hydrogen peroxide even removes the odor of pet accidents. And if you run out of hydrogen peroxide, try toothpaste, or bar soap worked into a thick, creamy lather. (HINT: Rub the bar directly on the stain, adding water slowly. If you're at a restaurant and spill, the dispenser soap works, too, but don't use a paper towel to rub it or the dyes in it may stain your garment.)

Rubber gloves quickly pick up even the most stubborn pet hair from chairs and clothes. (HINT: Sprinkle baby powder into the gloves to help your hand slide easily in and out.)

Use two wicker paper plate holders (one under and one above your food) when cooking in the microwave. This prevents hard-to-clean splatters in the oven and the holders also double as potholders or trivets for serving the food.

Peanut butter or rubbing alcohol will remove gum from practically anything.

Twist the air out of plastic grocery bags and tie them in a knot to store them compactly for reuse or recycling. Or roll them like commercially packaged bags and store them in an empty trash bag box for easy dispensing.

Automatic coffeemaker filters are great lint-free wipes at a fraction of the cost of paper towels (see Principle #8).

At the Office

Some of the ways you can use assembly-line principles on the job include: use form letters or paragraphs as much as possible; do all of your correspondence (or other like duties) at one time; schedule blocks of time to make all your telephone calls at once, when you are fresh; keep items to be photocopied in a folder and make fewer trips to the copy room each day; hold your mail and add postage at the end of the day; learn how to use computer macros and other timesaving features of your software programs.

Assembly-line principles not only save you time, but they alleviate a lot of stress. Assess your routine chores to see which can be done more efficiently in an assembly-line manner.

My process for Organization, The Way:

_____

_____

_____

_____

_____

_____

_____

_____

_____

_____

The Way is empty,
yet use will not drain it. . . .
Blunt the sharpness;
Untangle the knots;
Soften the glare;
Let your wheels
move only
along old ruts.

*Enthusiasm
bring
internal
happiness
and external
success.*

Principle Six:
Use time saving devices

From discovering fire, to making tools, to taming the horse, humans have continually journeyed toward efficient living. We have invented so many timesaving devices it would take pages to list them all. Aren't you glad you no longer have to wind up your car to start it? Or your phonograph? I can't imagine having to type and revise manuscripts in the days of manual typewriters and carbon paper. Microwaves and dishwashers have freed many from the kitchen. Computers have taken over the world.

Inventions are the result of someone getting so tired of doing something the slow, hard, manual way that they created a tool to alleviate the annoyance. If you want to be organized, you should invest in as many of these tools as you can afford. If there isn't a mechanical aid available to help with a task that annoys you, remember that anyone can be an inventor.

My Favorite Time Savers
Kitchen gadgets are my absolute downfall. I even travel with my Ginsu knife! Just remember, though, that some of these require more setup and cleanup time than what is saved by doing it manually.

Remote controls are wonderful—as long as you can find them. If you have several remotes, get one of the ready-made holders or a small wicker basket to keep them all in place by your favorite chair, and then develop a habit (see Principle #8) of putting them there when not in use.

Business cards are a much easier way to give your contact information to a new friend or business acquaintance than digging for pen and scratch paper. Business cards don't have to be fancy or costly. You can even make your own on the computer using preformatted paper found at office supply stores.

Another inexpensive timesaver is the rubber stamp. If you get the capped, self-inking kind, you can take it anywhere. Use rubber stamps for addressing envelopes to those you correspond with regularly. Make one up for approving invoices, with spaces for filling in the date, amount paid, account to be charged and the approval signature. (HINT: Red ink makes the information stand out on the page.) Use rubber stamps for mail coding. Stamping "First Class," "Special Fourth Class," "Parcel Post," etc. on an envelope is much faster than typing or handwriting it and usually speeds your letter through the postal system faster as well. Use rubber stamps for your return address, or self-adhesive labels. Either one comes in handy for entering sweepstakes and placing mail orders. Carry the labels or rubber stamp in your purse or pocket to quickly enter contests at conventions or stores. This helps avoid writer's cramp, too. They're also great for labeling books, tools, or other items you may lend to others.

Paper shredders save time and energy and protect your privacy. You can get small ones that fit right on your wastebasket for less than fifty dollars.

If you have a bad sense of direction, carry a compass. I have one that looks like a pocket watch, complete with a flip-up lid. That trusty little tool has many times saved me from driving miles in the wrong direction.

In the office, a simple sorter can save all kinds of time and energy when filing. Obtainable at any office supply company, sorters are labeled numerically, alphabetically, or by month.

My favorite and most used tool, however, is my kitchen timer. Factories use bells to signal ends of breaks, lunch periods and shifts. Sporting events use them to end a period of play. Even your local do-it-yourself car wash uses a warning bell when your time is about to run out. There is an important reason for this. If you don't have to keep an eye on the clock, you will be better able to focus on the task at hand. And as we've already covered, focusing helps you complete a task more efficiently.

I have a wonderful digital timer made by West Bend. I can set up to three separate times at once, from a few seconds to several hours of duration. And, because it is digital, I don't have to listen to the ticking of time running out. I don't just time my cooking projects (although it's indispensable there). I use it for everything and definitely carry it with me everywhere I go.

When I lived in an apartment with an on-site Laundromat, the timer allowed me to go back to my apartment and do other things while the clothes were washing and drying—without having to worry about forgetting to take them out (see Principle #9).

When I was working in offices and also writing, I wrote in the mornings, setting the timer for when I had to get ready for work. This left me free to concentrate and create, without having to worry about being late for my job.

Use a timer to signal when to leave for an appointment or other obligation. Set it for when a favorite television show comes on, when you must attend the staff meeting or when you need to make an important conference call. Use it on coffee breaks to enjoy every minute without worrying about returning late. I've avoided parking tickets by using my timer to monitor parking meters or remind me to move my car on street-cleaning days.

If you have trouble getting the kids off to school, use the timer instead of nagging. Tell them when the timer goes off the first time, they have ten minutes to gather their books and lunches and meet you at the door for their goodbye kiss. Reset it to signal that the school bus is due, or the carpool is leaving. The kids may be late the first couple of days, but if you leave without them, or they miss their morning kiss, or you threaten them with the return of the morning nag, it won't take long before you'll have a smooth-running morning. By letting children take the responsibility, you are not only teaching them a valuable life lesson, but everyone's day will go better by dispensing of the early-morning harangue.

In fact, a timer can be a powerful tool for teaching responsibility and setting limits in many areas. Allow children free playtime until the timer goes off to signal study time must begin. Tell them they must spend ten minutes cleaning their room or doing some other dreaded chore. If they work steadily until the timer goes off, they will get a reward. Use it to monitor your child's television-watching time. Want to call your favorite friend who lives on the other side of the world but you're afraid you'll talk for hours and your budget can't stand another $300 phone bill? Set the timer and make the call. When it goes off, say goodbye. Surfing the web is another activity that can eat up hours and may require a timer to regulate.

The list is endless, but you get the point. I even use it to regulate myself on my favorite hobby. Anyone who has ever put together a jigsaw puzzle will know what I mean when I say that hours can slip by unnoticed while you're engrossed in finding that piece that should be so easy to spot. Now I set the timer for whatever block of time I can spend. When it goes off, I get up and walk away. Well, most of the time!

One of the best uses for a timer, though, I think, is the power nap. Fifteen minutes of total relaxation can effectively rejuvenate even the most exhausted person, especially if you use a sleep mask to block all light from your eyes. Setting a timer frees you from keeping one eye on the clock, or worrying about missing an important obligation, and thereby provides that total relaxation. No, I haven't forgotten about the standard alarm clock, but I like the timer better because it's more quickly and easily set, and I don't have to worry about oversleeping because I forgot to reset the alarm for my morning wake-up time. You can use a timer in your office when the day starts to jangle. You don't even have to lie down. Just set the timer for five minutes and stare at your desk as if you are concentrating on proofing a report. No one will know and you'll keep your edge in a competitive world. If your job takes you on the road, even better. Pull over in a shaded park and give yourself a five-minute break. The time spent will be easily recovered by your increased enthusiasm and productivity.

Analyze your day and see where a timer can be used. You'll soon wonder how you ever got along without it.

Supply Kits for Home and Office

Having proper tools and supplies is a big key to saving time and being organized. There are several basic supply kits every home, office and car should have. Use boxes, baskets, or drawers to keep these frequently used items together and readily available. You can buy containers that are designed especially for these, or use tool boxes, makeup kits, fishing tackle kits, Tupperware containers, etc. The listed items are practical for almost everyone, but as usual adapt the suggestions to your personal needs.

Office Kit. In addition to some type of filing cabinet, drawer, or box for organizing papers and receipts, your office kit should include an inexpensive, preferably battery-operated calculator, extra batteries, writing paper, pens and pencils, #10 business envelopes, mailing labels, Scotch tape and mailing tape, a few large manila envelopes, highlighter pens, magic markers in several colors, scissors, stapler and staple-remover, pencil sharpener or lead for mechanical pencils, paper clips, rubber bands, and phone books. If you carry a supply of these items in your briefcase, you have a ready office-on-the-road (see Principle #8).

Medical Kit. Buy a ready-made kit, or make your own using a small box. Keep a variety pack of Band-Aids, cloth tape and gauze, hydrogen peroxide and/or rubbing alcohol, tweezers, nail clippers, an antiseptic cream like Neosporin, anti-itch cream like Benadryl, sunblock, bug spray, body lotion, Vaseline, and whatever medications you use, from simple aspirin to prescription drugs. If you live in the desert, include a snake bite kit.

Sewing Kit. Basic items include pins (straight and safety), needles (variety of sizes), needle-threader (this inexpensive little gadget can save all kinds of time), thread (black, white and any other basic color that dominates your wardrobe), small scissors, iron-on patches, a variety pack of snaps and other fasteners, a small roll of Velcro, and a measuring tape. If you actually sew, and not just repair, you'll undoubtedly expand this kit enormously.

Cleaning Kit. Basic necessities include a broom or sweeper, dust mop (if you have hardwood floors), toilet brush, small pail, an all-purpose cleaner, floor cleaner/wax, wet mop (unless you prefer the hands-and-knees method like I do), furniture polish, soap (body, dish and laundry), spray starch, glass cleaner, a feather duster and plenty of rags (old T-shirts work well). And don't forget the helpful hints in Principle #5: baking soda, hydrogen peroxide, and coffeemaker filters.

Surgical gloves are a must to protect your hands. These can be purchased in bulk at less cost than standard rubber gloves, and I like them better than the standard gloves because they aren't so clumsy to work with.

You can also add a plant mister, aquarium cleaners, shoe polish, etc. if they are practical for your lifestyle.

Car Kit. To alleviate travel worries, keep such items in your trunk as a first aid kit, a basic set of tools, flashlight, flares, lighter (the long-nosed butane kind can be purchased inexpensively in the sporting goods department of your local discount department store), moist towelettes, canned tire inflator, extra hoses and belts, black electrical tape, city and state maps, antifreeze and windshield cleaner, a quart of oil, jumper cables, emergency information, and coins for the phone or toll charges.

You may want to keep an extra copy of the telephone directory for your city since you can seldom find one in a phone booth anymore. If you're traveling in the desert or in any hot weather, it's a good idea to have a canteen or a jug of water along as well.

In winter climates, carry a blanket, scarf, gloves and a warm coat and boots, as well as tire chains. These items may save your life if a sudden blizzard strands you. I learned this lesson the hard way some years ago in Kansas. I had driven from Kansas City to Wichita for a concert on a Saturday. It was 70 degrees and sunny when my son and I started out in the morning, so we were dressed in shorts and light jackets. When we left the concert to drive home, freezing rain turned to snow. The temperature plummeted and visibility dropped to zero. The snow finally got so deep, we were forced to pull over to the side of the road. Fortunately, I did have a blanket in the trunk, which may have saved our lives. At the very least, it made us a little more comfortable until a snowplow passed and we could continue on to a hotel at the next exit.

Consider packing a small suitcase with a comfortable set of clothes and shoes for each member of the family (sweatsuit and sneakers or hiking boots at the very least), and keeping it in the trunk. If you have to flee in the night because of fire, earthquake or other sudden disaster, you will appreciate having comfortable clothes to wear for as long as the emergency lasts. Hopefully, you will never have to use any of these items, but if you do, you will be eternally grateful that they were available.

By the way, if you're short of room in your house, consider using your trunk to store your camping items. In case of an emergency, they can prove very helpful.

Hardware Kit. Include a flashlight, hammer, flathead and Phillips screwdrivers, a variety pack of nails and screws, glue, yardstick, measuring tape, staple gun with staples, candles, tape (electrical and masking), a can of WD-40, light bulbs, pliers, ball of string, lighter or matches, a utility knife, and a good adjustable wrench. Add drills and other power tools you have frequent use for.

If your means are limited, consider sharing larger tools and equipment with others. Pool your resources for a neighborhood Weedeater or chainsaw that can be passed around. Several times in my life my circle of friends has had a community vacuum cleaner. If you have a computer and your neighbor has a lawnmower, consider swapping computer work for lawn-mowing services.

Ah, yes, computers. The greatest timesaver of them all! We have invented a machine that performs just like our brains—only most of the time better. If you're a beginner, I strongly recommend formal instruction on any software program that you desire to use. Even the "...for Dummies" series of manuals often seem like gibberish to the novice, and classes explain and simplify even the most complex operations. They also allow you to learn from others' trials and errors, expose you to timesaving features you might not discover on your own, and more important, allow you time to experiment and practice, two important ingredients in discovering the most efficient way to use this valuable tool. A side benefit of attending classes is that you meet friends you can call on for support and with whom you can share computer horror stories.

One thing you'll notice, however, is that even though I am on the computer several hours every day, many of my suggestions are still manual. I just like having information available without having to power up a machine. And if your household has six people sharing one computer, it's definitely more efficient to do something manually than to wait your turn.

Reference Kit. Using reference books relieves your brain from retaining tedious information, freeing it up for more important matters. I believe it was Einstein who said a person should never try to remember something sheh can look up. There are several basic reference materials that should be in every home: recipe books, appliance manuals, a good dictionary, an atlas, and a Bible or other spiritual guidebook. Encyclopedias are especially helpful if you have school age children, and many publishers now put out interactive volumes on computer disk. If students can do their research at home, you save the time and energy of driving them to the library.

The Internet is probably the greatest reference resource you can ever have in your home. If you can't find the answer to your question on the Internet, you probably don't need to know the answer. Even so, it's handy to keep the old manual resources available, in case you're tenth in line for the computer and your inquiring mind wants to know something now.

Documents Kit. Even if you have a safety deposit box at your local bank, you should still keep certain papers and information in a locked, fireproof box in your home for easy reference and in case access to your bank is impossible. Papers to be included are insurance policies, wills, birth certificates, diplomas, passports, lease or mortgage papers, loan documents, and perhaps legal documents.

Compile a list of important financial information: policy numbers, amounts and agents for all insurance policies (don't forget those on charge accounts or through your bank), checking, savings and investment account numbers, balances and contact information, credit card and charge account numbers and contact information, social security/license/car registration information (extremely helpful when your wallet has been lost or stolen), and any other important asset or liability information you might have. If you are suddenly summoned to another plane of existence, your survivors will appreciate having this information available (see Principle #2).

Specialty Kit. There may be other kits that apply to your career or hobbies. A large, lightweight plastic toolbox is great for transporting the sundry supplies you'll need if you are, say, a caterer, an entertainer, or if you do freelance bartending or flower arranging.

You may already have most or all of the items for these kits scattered around the house. The trick to being organized is to collect them all in one box or area and keep them replenished. Examine every area of your life to discover how the proper tools and supplies can be organized to maximize your efficiency.

When you know
the mother
Go on
to know the child. . . .
To see the small
is called discernment;
To hold fast
to the submissive
is called strength.

*Every
individual
is in our olife
to teach us
to love
ourselves.*

Principle Seven:
Develop teamwork

Teamwork helps you be more organized in several ways. You can enlist the help of others to complete a task more quickly by splitting the workload. You can use the creative powers or experiences of others to find a better way to complete a task more efficiently yourself. If you have the authority, you can delegate time-consuming obligations and not have to do them at all, which can also be more cost-efficient. You can swap duties and errands with others to make better use of your time and theirs. For example, maybe one neighbor can make dry cleaning runs, one can drive children to school or other activities, and another one can pick them up.

Arranging progressive dinners (where you go to a different home for each course) or potluck meals can be a fun way to meet and know your neighbors or to fulfill several social obligations at once, easily and inexpensively. If you live in an ethnically diverse neighborhood, ask each person to bring a native dish. This provides a great opportunity to learn about other cultures (see below).

If you're home during the day, offer to be the drop-off place for package deliveries or service calls, or swap these time wasters with others, depending on individual schedules. If you don't have a car, ask your neighbor to run your errands while you clean or iron for hir.

Human resources, obviously, are one of the most important tools of being organized. Before you can work effectively with others, however, you must establish a good personal relationship with them.

Accept Others

Most of us learned the following concept at a young age: Do unto others as you would have others do unto you. But we forget the lesson as adults. How easy it is to treat others with respect, to smile and say "please"and"thank you"and yet how often these common courtesies are disregarded in our fast-paced society.

Spot check your actions toward others. Visualize your roles reversed, and adjust your actions accordingly. Ask yourself if you are reacting from love—or from fear. It's my philosophy that these are the only two reasons we do anything.

Go with the flow of others' moods. Every human being has good days and bad days. Most of the time the reasons have nothing to do with those around us. If the problem does lie with you, try to correct it. If there's nothing you can do about the situation, then don't take it personally. It's only your ego that feels it must defend itself against a perceived attack. Anger and bitterness are two factors that do nothing but get in the way of efficient action.

If someone you have to deal with is constantly in a bad mood, try to discover why. Does the battle-ax at work go home to an abusive relationship where sheh has no power? Is that why sheh wields hir authority in the workplace? Is that shy little person from the strict Catholic home insecure about hir sexuality so that's why sheh flirts so pathetically? Is a recently hired employee threatening your boss's position in the company, making hir fear being replaced and thus turning hir a slave into driver?

Once you've considered someone's actions in this light, you don't have to buy into hir adverse behavior. It will then cease to bother you. As the saying goes, "What you resist, will persist." Even if you don't find out the reasons for the unpleasant attitudes, by trying to understand, you will find yourself more accepting of others the way they are.

An enlightening book by Ken Keyes, Jr.—*Handbook to Higher Consciousness* (Living Love Publications, Coos Bay, OR, 1975)—lists twelve pathways to peace and happiness. The twelfth pathway says, "I am perceiving everyone, including myself, as an awakening being who is here to claim [hir] birthright to the higher consciousness planes of unconditional love and oneness."Repeating this to yourself can change a negative interaction into an accepting one simply by changing your perception.

If you think about it, you can probably recall a time when you acted in the same manner as the person who is irritating you now. Have you ever been in a hurry and inadvertently cut someone off in traffic? Maybe once? Or missed a chance to make a left turn because you were daydreaming? Well, maybe this is the only time in hir life that the offending driver has ever done the same thing. Do you know? Ultimately, "road rage"hurts you the most.

I came across an interesting little quiz one time, and if I still had it, I would include it here. Basically it set up several little scenarios and asked you to judge your reactions to them. Two I remember involved saying hello to someone who ignored you and almost being blown off the road by a speeding driver. The quiz then told you the why behind these incidents. In the first scenario, the person was hearing impaired; in the second, the person was driving a bleeding child to the hospital. Kind of changes the whole thing around, doesn't it?

Usually, if you can pinpoint the reason why something irritates you, you will discover an area in your own life that needs work. That's right. That annoying person is only mirroring what you refuse to recognize as a fault in yourself.

So don't give blame—or credit—to anyone else for the degree of happiness or unhappiness you are experiencing. You can't change others. But you can change your perception and your reaction.

Understand Cultures

As technology and trade make the world an ever smaller place, it is becoming increasingly important to understand the different cultures that make up our cities in order to understand the people we now encounter on a daily basis. We often hear about melting pots, but what if we instead consider ethnically diverse environments as tossed salads? Instead of expecting everyone to blend together, why not see each person as a separate, tasteful ingredient that retains hir uniqueness while creating a perfect whole?

I remember reading some years back about three young girls who were caught smoking in high school and sent to the principal's office. Two of the girls were let off with a reprimand and detention, but one was expelled. There was naturally an uproar, since the girl who was dismissed was of a different culture than the majority of the school's population. When asked why only the one girl was disciplined so harshly, the principal cited disrespect as the reason: The girl had refused to look at him during the entire disciplinary meeting and the principal said this indicated the girl's insolence and lack of remorse. When an informed counselor intervened and explained that, in the girl's culture, lack of eye contact with an authority figure is actually the highest form of respect, the girl was quickly reinstated.

I think of that incident every time I interact with someone from a different background. It is important for each of us to consider the ruling ethics, mores, and body language, etc. of the various cultures with which we come into contact. Only then will we all get along as a world family.

After the LA riots, there were suggestions for community meetings to exchange such cultural information as a way of healing and preventing such tragedies. I don't know how much of this has actually been done, but it was a wonderful suggestion. There are museums now that do this, too, such as the Museum of Tolerance in Los Angeles. Schools are finding entertaining ways to foster an exchange of knowledge, not only about different races but also differing lifestyles based on economic, social, or religious factors. It gives me hope that someday we truly will all be one.

But let's not leave it up to others. If you live down the street from a family from a different culture, invite them to dinner. Ask them about their background and be genuinely interested in their answers. You might be surprised that you're not far apart on the basics. Or, as mentioned above, plan a potluck event that includes the various ethnic groups and dishes.

Don't Overcommit

There are times when you shouldn't go with the flow if you want to be organized. By accepting or volunteering for every job offered, you overwhelm yourself and stymie efficient action. You must learn to say no.

If someone continually comes to you for solutions to problems, don't just automatically give them the answer. Instead, encourage them to solve the dilemma themselves. Ask them questions to steer them toward a viable alternative. If you do offer a solution, explain how you arrived at it. If they understand the rationale behind the suggested action, they will be able to apply it to future problems without involving you. And remember, people respond better if you point out what's right rather than what's wrong. If you must correct or criticize, word it positively.

Another time you must tactfully call a halt is when someone is wasting your time with idle chatter. This happens frequently on the job. You may be rushing to get a report done and Jack wants to tell you—for the third time—every detail of the house he's made an offer on. Or Mary is upset because her latest lover has just told her he's getting married next week-to someone else! Be firm but not rude. Calmly explain you can't talk right now. Smile. Suggest lunch. Or listen for a minute, express your sympathy, then go about your task, letting your body language say that you are no longer available to listen. Once the person realizes they have lost your full attention, they will usually stop talking. A little small talk is necessary for maintaining effective working relations, but you must know when to cut it off.

This advice applies especially to negativity and complaining. First make sure you're not the one being negative. If something can be done about a situation, do it. If not, accept it and go on. If another person tries to waste your time with complaints, let them vent for a minute and then offer a positive spin on the situation if you can. If the carping continues, say kindly but firmly, "I'm sorry, but I refuse to give a bad situation any energy by discussing it or even listening to it." Smile and offer this in a nonjudgmental tone and you may change someone's life.

E-mail is another major time waster in today's society. I love e-mail and it allows me to stay in touch with friends everywhere, but we must not let ourselves be a slave to it. At work, where your employer is paying for your time, e-mailing that is out of hand is actually stealing from the company. (HINT: Be careful what you write in personal e-mails from the office. The information is retained in several different files, and it may not be deleted, even when you empty the recycle bin on your desktop.)

The same time wasting applies to telephones. I think answering machines are possibly the greatest invention of the century. I leave mine on constantly and screen all my calls. I may love my friends, but when I am far away in the world of creativity, even a quick hello can jar me out of it and destroy a whole day of writing. And I'm sure anyone who has ever had dinner interrupted by a telemarketer appreciates the benefit of an answering machine or service. Again, time spent on personal calls from the job is robbing your employer of time he is paying for. If you don't think you're an offender, keep track of the time spent on personal calls for one week. You may be shocked. Another factor to consider is that if you are tying up a line with a personal phone call, a moneymaking call may not get through to your employer, which could adversely affect your job security.

Learning to say no applies in the home as well. Don't pick up after everyone in the house. Teach your children by example. Don't nag. Expect.

I like to keep my house very neat. Even my messes are in orderly piles. When my son was growing up, however, things weren't so easy to keep straightened up. He'd drop his jacket, toys or schoolbooks wherever he happened to be. I'd yell. The result was stress for both of us. When he was about six, we sat down and talked about it. Finally we designated his room as off-limits to my neatness obsession. He understood that if I found anything of his in the common areas of the house I would pick it up and throw it in the door of his room, to fall where it may. The door stayed shut so I didn't have to explain the room's devastation to visitors, and I didn't have to look at it. Nor did I have to clean it. That became his responsibility.

It worked beautifully. Areas of the house in which I operated were up to my standards without a fight, and I had eliminated one room from my weekly cleaning schedule. The amazing thing was that Jon quickly realized how things could pile up if not attended to. He began to be annoyed with having to walk over and around things scattered on the floor, with clearing his bed before he could crawl into it, and apologizing to his guests because the room was such a mess. Soon he started putting things away on his own, dusting, doing his own laundry. Eventually, when he was in high school and my consulting business kept me so busy I let my housekeeping standards slip, Jon began cleaning the rest of the house when he did his room. I swear. Without being asked!

Enlist your family's help with household chores. Assign everyone certain duties. If you rotate them weekly or monthly, everyone can learn how to do each task and no one has to worry about getting stuck with the worst job forever. Make up charts and post them. These can act as check-lists so no one can say, "Oh, I forgot about that." Not only does this lighten your workload, but it also teaches your child practical life lessons.

Because in many families both parents are now working outside the home, it is sometimes helpful if kids do more than their share. Many schools of parenting insist on giving allowances that are not tied to duties, which are assigned and expected. I disagree. Why not teach the work ethic from an early age? Instead of free allowances or assigned duties (or perhaps in addition to them), set up a work chart for every household task a child can complete. Down the left side of the chart, list each duty and its wage rate. To the right, set up a column for each day of the week, as well as a total column. If you have several children, make a separate chart for each of them, with chores based on their age and skill level. For older children, if you include chores like cleaning the refrigerator or oven, weeding the garden, or doing the laundry, there is the added bonus of their learning how to do things they'll need to do when they are out on their own. Let the children know they don't have to do any of these duties, but if they don't they will have no spending money.

Throughout the week, as chores are completed, the children should put a checkmark under the appropriate day and chore. Every Saturday, sit down with your child and calculate together the salary to be paid. This provides a simple, visual lesson of the work ethic that a million words could not teach. Add a little praise for jobs well done, and it becomes an important time for building self-esteem.

The bonus to your efficiency is that once the children realize the money they have the potential to make, there are very few chores left for you to do.

See the Big Picture

Another way you can be more efficient when working with others is to know what they do. Know something about your neighbors' schedules so you don't bother a night shift worker during hir prime, daytime sleeping period. Find out meal times so you don't call and interrupt what is hopefully—ideally—a family time.

At your office, study the organizational chart. Understand how your department fits into the organizational structure. If you send paperwork to other departments, find out what happens to it there. Are there things you can do to simplify someone else's job? If you show a willingness to make things easier for others, they'll generally return the favor.

I remember when I worked at Holiday Kitchens, a Wisconsin manufacturer of kitchen cabinets. My job was to type the orders and give them to the shop foreman for distribution throughout the factory. The order form had several color-coded copies. After the order was typed, I'd keep two of the copies and staple the remaining ones together for the shop. One day, while walking through the factory in search of the "big picture," I noticed the foreman sitting at his desk working on the huge stack of orders I'd just sent out to him. He was removing each staple and rearranging the colored copies into a sequence that was more efficient for distribution. I immediately realized that if I simply stapled them in a new sequence (which actually proved easier for me), I would save him an enormous amount of time—not to mention aggravation. For years he had daily seethed while doing that one tedious little task, but he hadn't said anything because he didn't want to burden the typist. Boy, did I make his day!

So speak up. Work with other departments, not against them. If your company does not currently do so, suggest monthly meetings or a company newsletter to solicit comments or advice on everyone's work area and to share morale-boosting stories. You can discuss how paperwork can be streamlined. Help each other over hurdles. Look for duplications that can be eliminated.

Another way to foster teamwork in your place of employment is to remove the statement, "It's not my job" from your vocabulary. Believe me, the time you'll save by helping others comes back tenfold. Again, however, don't overdo it by becoming a crutch for a manipulative or lazy coworker.

In addition to studying the organizational chart on your job, you can increase your teamwork factor by reading the company's bio and your boss's resume and job description. Do outside reading about your company's industry. This goes back to building your database and planning ahead (see Principle #2), and we've already discussed how that improves your efficiency. It can also earn you raises. For instance, passing on to your employer an article from a magazine sheh might not read could give hir the edge in a business transaction and earn the company dividends. Or save your company from disaster. (HINT: If this happens, be sure to make a note in your Things-To-Do Diary [see Principle #4] so you remember to use it to support your next raise request.)

When you are learning a new job, it is important that you understand exactly what your job duties are. Equally important is to understand why things are done the way they are. Understanding the logic behind something not only helps you remember what to do, but allows you to think through to solutions when you hit a snag. If explanations are not offered, ask for them. If you're doing the training, explain the rationale as you describe the duty.

Make Meetings Efficient

As already mentioned, meetings are good places to set departmental and company goals, foster teamwork, and review progress. But they must be run efficiently.

If you are in charge, keep meetings short and organized. Prepare a written agenda and distribute it a day or two before the meeting. This allows employees to consider what questions they have or what input they want to offer. Set time limits on discussions (use the handy kitchen timer introduced under Principle #6). Start the meetings on time. It amazes me how our society punishes the people who are prompt to meetings by making them wait for those who are late. I've attended several meetings recently where the doors were shut and no one was allowed to enter after the scheduled start time. That may be too drastic a measure, since we all sometimes have unavoidable reasons for arriving late, but meetings should definitely begin on time and should not be interrupted to acknowledge latecomers or catch them up on what they've missed.

If your meetings are not handled in this manner, volunteer to help run them. If that's not possible, then don't waste your waiting time. Read a book, organize your day, proof a report, discuss a problem with a co-worker, or take a mini-mind-trip to Cozumel or to your ideal day as envisioned under Principle #1. Do something constructive with the time.

Schedule Time Off

To be an effective team player, you must be dependable. Be where

71

you're supposed to be when you're supposed to be there, and others will be more likely to return the courtesy. Plan your vacations, lunch periods, doctors'appointments, and so forth around slow times, or times convenient to your boss's and coworkers'schedules.

If someone will be covering your position while you are gone, leave a written list of where to find things and how to do the various tasks required. On every job I've had, I've set up a three-ring binder of itemized instructions on how to complete every job duty. Some employees seem to feel that secrecy about what they do gives them job security, but a written description can actually increase your value. Not only does it show your employer exactly how much you really are responsible for, but it shows you care about your position and the company. In fact, if I were an employer, I would insist on this as a condition for the employee's first raise, even if a previous employee has already done one. This ensures the instructions are updated in case the employee gets hit by the proverbial truck. Such a job description also provides good insight into whether the employee actually understands what sheh is doing.

If you have been on vacation or sick leave, don't forget to say thank you to whomever handled your workload while you were gone, preferably in writing, or with a flower from your garden or a token gift.

If you cover for someone else, keep extra copies of all letters and memos sent or received, notes on phone calls or meetings; in other words, keep some kind of written record of everything that was done while you were in charge. This will allow the employee to easily get back up to speed when they return. Use manila folders to sort the paperwork, using such categories as: things done, things on hold, mail received, things to do, etc.

Create a Think Tank

Successful businesspersons have discovered the value of think tanks. These are groups of people who combine their creative abilities to solve problems or find better ways to do things. They can be set up in almost any size, for almost any endeavor. Evaluate the benefits of a think tank in your organization.

Solicit a Mentor

Along the same lines, find a person you respect and admire—

someone who is successful (materially and/or spiritually) in whatever area you want to succeed in. Make an appointment to meet with them to solicit their advice. Even the busiest executive will usually find time to share hir knowledge with an individual who sincerely and considerately seeks it. (HINT: Be sure to send a thank you.)

Respect Confidences

Though the confidences you hold may not make headline news if released, the surest way to eliminate helpful partners is to run your mouth about their private affairs.

Properly utilizing the human resources around us not only makes us more efficient but adds the element of good relationships to make us a success.

In the
pursuit of learning
one knows more every day;
In the pursuit
of The Way
one does less every day.
One does less
and less
until one does nothing at all,
And when
one does nothing at all
there is nothing
that is undone.

*What you
give out,
you get back.
It's the law of
the Universe.*

*Principle Eight:
Develop harmonious habits*

Habits have gotten a bad rap. Our first thoughts when we hear the word *habits* seem to be of bad things: smoking, drinking, drugs, biting our fingernails, frowning. Hardly ever do we think of good habits like eating healthily, hanging up our bath towel, or sharing our wealth. But the word *habit* comes from the Latin *habere*, which means, "to have, to hold." Habits, then, are those things that we hold as our own; those practices we have found to be of value.

As mentioned at the beginning of this book, anything consciously practiced for twenty-one days becomes a habit. The wonderful thing about habits is that once you are accustomed to doing them, they become almost automatic. Not having to make decisions on how to do something speeds up the whole process of action.

Most of the suggestions in this book can become habitual processes. Here are a few more harmonious habits that can help you organize your life. Again, these are offered as guidelines to be altered to individual needs and personality and to inspire you to create your own habits to remove petty time wasters from your life.

Put Things Away

Get in the habit of putting things back in their place the minute you stop using them. It may take a few seconds longer now to walk over

75

and put the scissors away, but the next time you need them, it will take a lot less time to go straight to the drawer or pencil holder than to run around in circles looking for them.

This works for any item you use consistently—your jewelry, phone book, briefcase, the dictionary, and especially your keys. If you've ever had to look for your keys when you're already late for an appointment, you know the frustration. Ask yourself, "If I needed to get my keys in my hand within ten seconds in order to win a million dollars right this minute, where would I look for them first?" Trust your first impulse. That is the place your keys should be placed every time they're not in use—a peg by the door, a bowl on the entry table, your purse, or a drawer in the kitchen. Now, for the next twenty-one days, consciously remind yourself to immediately put your keys in that spot every time you finish with them. Stick up Post-it note reminders if you have to. At the end of that time, you should not only never have to hunt for lost keys again, but you will realize you're not even having to think about putting the keys in their spot. In fact, if you forget to put them there, you will feel a nagging in the back of your brain that something is not right.

Another related problem people have with keys is locking them in the car. Talk about throwing a schedule into chaos. To avoid this ever happening again, develop the habit of immediately pulling the keys from the ignition as you turn off the car. Make it all part of the same movement of turning the key so that, if you don't do it, your body will automatically signal you that something is wrong. Locking car doors while driving and when leaving the car is another sensible habit to get into doing. Also, buckling your seatbelt. Again, make these a habitual part of the process of closing the car door and you'll be triggered by an incomplete feeling should you forget.

A bonus of putting things back is neatness and neatness works psychologically to make you more organized. When everything has its place and everything is in its place, you will automatically feel that you have more control over your environment and situations that arise. Of course the effectiveness of the neatness habit is directly proportional to how many members of your household or office have developed it. But do it anyway. Every little bit helps, and your example might just inspire others to follow suit.

Pack Ahead

Have you ever arrived at a meeting out of the office and discovered you've forgotten an important paper? Have you ever been away from your home or office and realized you needed a phone number you forgot to bring? The habit needed to avoid this problem is to pack ahead.

For example, about a week before a scheduled long-distance trip, set out a suitcase in an out-of-the-way place (or if there's no space, designate a corner in which to begin a pile). Now, sit down and imagine yourself during every moment of your trip. See yourself having the most fun you've ever had, meeting the person of your dreams, or getting that important account. As the pictures float across your mind's movie screen, make a list of every piece of clothing and personal item you see yourself wearing. That's what you'll be packing. Consider also a sudden rainstorm, or other change of plans, and decide what will make that problem more bearable.

From this point until you leave on your trip, as you launder items or use them for the last time before you depart, immediately put them into the suitcase and check them off the list. On the day of departure, when you have only the few last-minute items to add and a list to remind you what those items are, you won't have to panic and you won't forget a thing.

If you travel frequently, keep travel-size supplies of personal items and/or cosmetics in your suitcase. You may even want to designate certain clothing for travel only (a duplicate workout suit, for example) and keep them packed. This practice helps you avoid the tedium of packing from scratch each time and also ensures that you won't forget necessary items.

The practice of packing ahead also works for things you routinely need with you. Women are fortunate to have purses. In them we can carry all the items we can't live without for a moment—lipstick, tissue, nail clipper or file, appointment book, credit cards, business cards, address book, checkbook. We never have to think about gathering these things together when we leave the house.

If you prefer to carry a small purse or don't carry one at all, use a separate book bag, briefcase, backpack, or duffel bag for heavier items. Items I carry in mine include a camera, business-card wallet, cleaning supplies for my glasses, tape measure, sunglasses, and two small notebooks (one for notes and ideas and one to keep track of any cash I spend). The good thing about carrying this separate bag is that I can also add videos or library books to be returned as soon as I finish them so the next time I go to town I don't forget them. This was especially useful when I lived in Marble Canyon, Arizona and the nearest town was fifty miles away. The bag is also useful for carrying small purchases home. No more juggling a million things from the car to the house.

If you're relying on pockets to carry your essentials, get in the habit of emptying them in the same place each time you come home, preferably on the bureau near your closet. This way, as you put on your next outfit, you can make it a part of the process to put those things back into your pockets.

If you use a briefcase, get the larger square kind. It's as easy to carry as the thin ones and prevents overstuffing, which makes it much easier to work with. Keep a supply of standard items in the briefcase—pens and pencils (with extra lead if mechanical), paper clips, envelopes, address labels, business cards, small stapler with staples, Scotch tape, extra batteries for your recorder, a resume, reference or publicity materials, and one or two legal pads or notebooks. Anything that must go from your home to your office, or vice versa, should be kept in your briefcase when you are not working on it or be put in there the minute you decide it is needed.

As you schedule appointments, immediately put into the briefcase any materials required for the meeting. By making it a habit to use your briefcase as a collecting point, you won't have to worry about remembering six different papers or files at the last minute. All you have to remember is one briefcase that you leave sitting by the door and automatically take with you everywhere you go. No more last-minute panic.

When I was catering, I kept a backpack filled with items I might need on the job—two sets of bow ties, cummerbunds and cufflinks (in case something happened to one), moist towelettes, pen, pencil and paper (always a must for writers), perfume, sample sizes of makeup, travel-size baby powder (to feel fresh after setup), nail polish, first-aid items (Tylenol, Band-Aids, Neosporin, Campho-Phenique, Visine, 4-Way Nasal Spray), safety pins, a needle and small spools of black and white thread, a pumice stone (great for getting ink or stubborn dirt off your hands), an orange stick for cleaning my nails, hair-ties, hair spray, a long-nosed, butane lighter, a pair of black socks and comfortable black shoes, camera and extra roll of film, and a book (which often helped to break the tedium of waiting for the last guest to leave so we could finish with the cleanup or for the first guest to arrive when we were all set up). In cooler weather, I carried leggings and a thermal underwear shirt because I knew for me being cold led to being grouchy which led to blowing a tip.

I can't tell you how many times this habit saved the day. A co-worker forgot her cummerbund and borrowed my extra. No matches could be found to light the chafers and my lighter saved the day. The roll of film earned us a big tip when a client ran out of film halfway through her son's bar mihtzva. The Campho-Phenique was a lifesaver for a girl stung by a bee. An extra cufflink served as a replacement for a missing button on a waiter's shirt. I've gotten the reputation of being the one to come to for just about anything. I may not be a hero, but I find great pleasure in saving the day in a mundane way.

You can follow this same principle with your gym bag, school bag, toolbox, or for any other situation that requires that supplies be brought along.

Clean As You Go

There are several harmonious habits you can develop to make your housekeeping take less time and go more smoothly.

If you have a glass shower door, keep a short-handled rubber squeegee in the shower, and as soon as you turn off the water, whisk away the drops to prevent them from drying into ugly water spots. Wipe off the sink counter each time you use it and the mirror while it is steamed over from the shower. The coffee filters mentioned in Principle #5 work great for this. Keep a supply in a drawer or under the bathroom sink. It also saves steps to keep extra bottles of glass and porcelain cleaners in the bathroom. You'll be more apt to use them regularly if you don't have to walk to the kitchen for them, and it might even encourage the rest of the family to use them as well.

Doing the dishes immediately after a meal (or at least loading them into the dishwasher) makes the task seem less burdensome because you don't have to waste time dreading doing it. I find, too, that the exercise of leisurely putting things away after a meal helps food digest better and banishes after-meal sluggishness.

If you have a large party that lasts late into the night, cleaning provides a leisurely wind down period as you savor the fun you've just had. If you're a morning person, however, just put away the food items and do the remainder of the cleanup in a broad sweep the following morning, when you're fresh and energetic. Whenever you do the cleanup, begin by going through the entire area with two garbage bags in hand (one for trash, one for recyclable items). You'll be amazed at how manageable the job looks once these items are gone. Next go through with a tray or dish-pan and collect items to be washed. If you have a dishwasher, these can be washing while you dust and clean the glass and floors. Or let the dishes soak while you're doing the dusting and floors so they will be easier to clean when you return to them.

There are many other ways cleaning as you go makes having an orderly house a breeze. Wipe up spills on your carpet or upholstery with a spot remover as soon as they occur. Dust while you're talking on the phone. Wipe off counters, stoves, tables, and refrigerators before spills can dry. If you can't wash dishes immediately, at least rinse them off, or fill them with water to prevent food from hardening on them. If you have an especially dirty pan, soak it for a few hours, or overnight, in soapy water. While you're waiting for your morning coffee to drip through the cof-feemaker, wipe off the refrigerator. While you're waiting for the water to boil for your pasta, clean the microwave. Stolen moments of cleaning are hardly noticeable and not only do they keep your house looking acceptable in case unexpected company stops by, but they make the big cleaning day a little easier to take.

Don't Hurry, Don't Worry

Haste makes waste, and worry dissipates energy. Develop the habit of keeping your attention focused on what you are doing, and maintain-ing a steady pace at the fastest speed you can achieve without stress. Develop a rhythm in your work, and you will find the Tao of doing it.

Take about ten minutes right now and try to remember one time when worrying had a positive effect on a situation. I guarantee you will not find one. Has worrying about a deadline ever once helped you beat it?

No. Has worrying about paying a bill ever helped you pay it? No. Has worrying about a disease, ever kept it from your body? No, although it may have invited a disease into your body.

In being organized, as with anything else, the negative energy generated by worrying actually works against the positive energy needed to accomplish the task at hand. Worry slows you down, stresses you out, and prevents life from being the fun it is meant to be. In fact, because negative thoughts are always at cross-purposes to efficiency, worry is the most destructive element to being organized.

Now I don't mean concern. Concern about a situation is healthy and usually necessary for finding a solution. Worry, on the other hand, is concern that becomes so obsessive it paralyzes our actions. Thus it is utterly useless in helping us accomplish anything. When you have tried everything you can think of and there is absolutely nothing you can do to change a situation, why continue to pound your head against the wall?

Worrying is a habit that can be broken when you no longer value it. I know this because I suffered from chronic hives all through childhood and developed an ulcer at the age of nineteen, all because of worry. Since I have finally gotten over it, not only do I no longer suffer from either of these, but my entire life has changed to one of glorious expectation. There are several ways you can learn not to worry. Visualize yourself five years into the future. Will this trauma that plagues you now really matter to you then? So why let it bother you today?

Use your own personalized trigger statement to blow off obstacles you can do nothing about. "Don't Worry, Be Happy" was the title of a popular song that became a catch phrase of comfort. Find something that is useful to repeat when you hear that fearful voice of worry talking in your brain. Or make up your own mantra. One I use is, "Oh, well . . ." Said with a drawl, a roll of the eyes, a shrug and a smile, it signifies my disappointment, acceptance and optimism concomitantly. "Whatever . . . " is another one.

I've always had a catch phrase to remind myself to keep things in perspective. I've used the ones above and many others. Currently I rely on "There's a reason for everything and all timing is set by the universe." If a person really believes that, as I do, how can sheh worry? Find a phrase that gives you the peace you deserve and use it.

Another thing you can do to banish worry is to ask yourself the question, "What is the worst thing that could happen if . . . and how would I deal with it?" You'll quickly see that no matter what happens, you will somehow find a way to cope, as you always have in the past. As long as you're still breathing, you are okay at this moment and have been okay so far.

Habits can be positive tools in our lives, but they are not learned overnight. As with everything else, practice makes perfect. If you have trouble remembering to practice the desired habit for the twenty-one days it takes to make it a part of your life, write yourself reminders on Post-it notes and stick them up everywhere. I know you'll find the rewards of having harmonious habits more than make up for the discipline required to foster them.

My steps for achieving Harmony:

_____

_____

_____

_____

_____

_____

_____

_____

_____

_____

_____

In a home
it is the site that matters;
In quality of mind
it is depth that matters;
In an ally
it is benevolence that matters;
In speech
it is good faith that matters;
In government
it is order that matters;
In affairs
it is ability that matters;
In action
it is timeliness
that matters.

*Be open
to this second:
what it can bring
to you and
what you can
bring to it.*

Principle Nine: Honor time

In one area of living—time—humankind has always been equal. We all have 86,400 seconds in every day. So why do some people seem to get more accomplished in life than others do? The answer is simple: They honor time by giving it value and using it wisely. They appreciate every moment and organize every hour. There are several ways to avoid wasting time. Here are just a few.

Let Your Fingers Do the Walking

Get in the routine of using the phone book to look up addresses, plan your routes, and to call ahead to avoid needless disappointment and wasted time. Write frequently used numbers in your personal phone book or Rolodex system; include places like your child's school, your hairdresser, the freight company, or post office.

Under the heading of "Video" in your Rolodex system, list the various video shops at which you are a member. If you are looking for a specific movie, you have all the numbers in one place and can call ahead. If the tape is available, ask the clerk to hold it at the desk to save even more time. (HINT: As you see previews or hear about movies you'd like to see, write them on a list that you keep in your wallet. This can save tons of time making a decision at the video store.)

Make a "Theater" listing in your address book or Rolodex system as well. With all the numbers in one place, you can quickly call around and check listings and show times. Or, if your city has a central number for movie listings, keep that number handy, as well as notes on the electronic menu choices to get to your information quickly. In malls, use the directories to find the stores you want to visit and go directly to them. (This can also save you money.) When looking for a particular item you want to purchase, use advertising flyers and the telephone to locate and price compare.

Combine Activities

One of the biggest time wasters in the American home today is the television. But television is also good for teaching, for keeping us abreast of the world around us, and for just plain relaxing after a hard day.

Television is a spectator sport, which means you can do other things while watching it and not miss a thing. Try organizing your recipe box or toolbox. Put photos into albums. Give yourself a manicure or a pedicure. Balance your checkbook. Open your mail. Any tedious task can be combined with your television viewing.

Television also helps make a dreaded project seem not so bad. Maybe it's the delicious feeling of breaking the childhood rule of having to do homework first before being able to watch television that turns doing something you have to do into something you want to do when you work on it in front of the television. Or it could be that the white noise of the set helps us focus.

Whether it's waiting on hold or gabbing with a best friend, telephone calls can be another big time waster. We've already discussed regulating telephone use with your answering machine (see Principle #6). But you can also combine the time you do spend on the phone with other activities, especially when using cordless or speaker phones. I love to dust while I'm on the telephone. It doesn't interfere with my attention on the conversation and keeps at least the surface layer of my house looking presentable. Manicures, pedicures, folding clothes, sorting tools and hardware are other suggestions. Anything that does not distract you from what the other person is saying. And don't be afraid to say goodbye and hang up once everything has been said.

Don't have time to exercise? Combine it with your daily endeavors. For example, when you go to the market, park at the far corner of the lot and walk briskly to the store. If the lot is busy, it'll probably take you less time to walk anyway.

When shopping, doing household chores, or reaching for things at the office, exaggerate your stretching and always bend from the waist. While you're waiting for your computer document to print or the Internet to connect, clasp your hands above your head and bend your arms right and left. There are many exercises you can do while sitting and driving. In fact, exercise can be slotted in almost anywhere. Of course, if you develop the habit of rising a half-hour earlier than usual to walk, jog, or do calisthenics or yoga, that's even better.

Do you love working crossword puzzles but feel they take time that could be better utilized doing other things? Do them in the bathroom. Reading is also a good bathroom activity. (HINT: If you are a one-bathroom family, be sure to take the timer with you, or at least set a limit of one sweep through the clues or one chapter in the book per visit.)

Don't Wait, Read

As long as there are books and magazines in the world, there is no reason to waste a single minute. Reading is probably the least expensive, easiest way to educate ourselves—but certainly one of the most neglected. "I don't have time to read," you lament. Well, guess what? No one has time to do anything; they take time to do what's important to them.

Waiting is probably the most tedious activity—or non-activity— we ever do. But those small pockets of time offer the perfect opportunity to read. Take a look at your day and see all the wasted moments that exist. Then pick up a book or magazine and carry it with you. Commit to reading an article or section of a book before you go to bed at night, or before you get up. Carry a book with you when traveling. Instead of stewing when traffic is at a standstill or the airplane bounces through rain, you can savor the time to devour the written word. Rather than standing in line waiting to board or disembark from public transportation, stay seated and read until the aisle has cleared.

How about reading while you eat lunch? Discovering an exciting new idea over the noon hour is incredibly effective in warding off an early-afternoon slump. Take a book with you when you go to the doctor's, hairdresser's, or auto mechanic's. Take one to the theater and get in a few minutes of reading while waiting in the ticket line, and a few more in the auditorium before the show starts. You'll soon find that reading instead of waiting alleviates the stress of downtime.

One way to best utilize the time you do take to read is to learn how to speed read. There are many books and classes on the subject. If you have trouble reading, consider taking a remedial reading class offered through local schools. And practice. Remember—no one has ever mastered anything without practice. Not even Einstein!

Even if you're on a tight budget, there is no excuse not to read. You can print articles on almost any subject off the Internet, and you can get almost any book at a library for only the cost of the time and gas you used to get there.

Use Reference Resources

To find library materials more efficiently, learn how to use the card catalogs or computerized directories available. You can look things up by title, author, and subject. Library personnel are happy to assist you.

Make use of the reference librarian as well. That's why sheh is there. It would be a boring job if nobody asked for help. Many times a reference librarian has answered in seconds a question I probably would have spent hours researching. Reference librarians are also available by phone. Some have direct lines; some you reach by calling the library's main number and asking for the reference desk. It's amazing how the persons who staff these lines have ready answers to an incredible range of questions, or can put their fingers on the information in seconds.

Don't forget about specialized university libraries. A college religious library reference desk, for instance, will probably be able to respond to your biblical question much more quickly than the general library reference personnel. Call a law library about your legal question.

When using a reference service, ask the librarian's name and use it. People are much more willing to help a person than a voice, a friend than a stranger. And willingness to act improves the speed of action. And don't forget the "thank you."

Handle Paperwork Quickly

Handle every piece of paper only once if at all possible. Look at the document, decide what needs to be done with it, do it, and then file the paper. If you file or discard each paper as you finish with it, or at least once a day, you will avoid having backlogged filing stack up so high it becomes a task you just can't face. Besides, if you need to find a copy of that paper in a hurry, it's a lot quicker to locate it in an organized file than to sift through a two-foot pile of papers for it.

For instance, when I go shopping, I put all my receipts in with my money as I receive them. Then, when I get home, I pull them out, post them and file them immediately. It literally takes seconds, and I never have to face a stack of papers to be dealt with, dread April 15, or search frantically for a receipt for a tax audit.

When filing, don't forget to cross-file if necessary. In other words, if someone asked to see that piece of paper, would they ask for it by the signature name, the company name, or the project name? If you're not sure, file a copy under each of the three.

If you can't decide where to file something, visualize being given the "Find it in ten seconds for a million dollars" test. Where is the first place you would look for the paper? That's where it should be filed.

Bring Business In-House

Consider holding business luncheons in your office as much as possible. Food can be ordered in for delivery and served restaurant-style at a small table in your office or in a private conference room. Order several different dishes to serve as a mini-smorgasbord on the plate. (HINT: Ask the guest for a food preference when you set the appointment to avoid food allergies or dislikes.)

The advantages of in-office luncheons are immediately evident. You don't have to drive to another part of town so you can work until the scheduled meeting time. There is no time wasted waiting for a table and ordering. There are no interruptions while discussing business, you don't have to worry about anyone overhearing confidential information, and files and other materials are readily at hand if you need them, without having to cart them all over town.

89

Use a tape recorder to keep the minutes of your meeting rather than a stenographer. One word of caution, be sure everyone attending is aware you are doing so. Send a copy of the transcription to each participant, retaining the original tape in case there are questions or misunderstandings.

Get to the Point and Don't Belabor It

Have you ever asked someone a simple question, received the answer in the first couple of words, and then had to listen to that person ramble on for five minutes, restating the answer in a zillion different ways? Talk about a time waster—for everyone involved. Scarcity increases value, so use words sparingly to give your thoughts maximum impact.

It is important to have our message understood, but repeating ourselves ad nauseam isn't effective. In fact, it can actually be counterproductive because the listener may get bored and zone out. It's better to relay the message, ask the other person to repeat it back, clarify and confirm the interpretation, and move on.

On the other hand, when you're receiving a message or instructions, don't be afraid to ask questions in order to understand the communication. Then write the information down so you don't have to be told again. The only dumb questions are the ones you've already been told the answers to or ones that are irrelevant to the subject at hand.

To correct the habit of overexplaining, record a few of your random conversations—at home, work, and especially on the telephone. Play them back and listen carefully. Make a conscious effort to think first before you speak in the future. (Okay, I confess that my friends will tell you this is one area where I definitely need work. But the important thing is, I am working on it!)

Maximize Errand Time

To lessen the time and stress spent running errands, combine several small trips into one big, circular route. Use a map if necessary, and consider the timing. For instance, if you have a whole day's worth of errands, stop for lunch before or after the lunch rush (before 11:30 or after 2:00 p.m.). It will be a quick but refreshing break. Stop at the shoemaker's sometime other than when the school's letting out next door. Plan your stops in advance and jot them down on a Post-it note in the order you will make them. Stick the note on your dashboard to keep you on course.

If you can, schedule flexible errands at odd times. Do your grocery shopping at 6:00 a.m. on Sunday mornings when you don't have to waste one moment waiting in line or maneuvering around other carts. If you're a night person, find a twenty-four-hour market and shop at 2:00 a.m. (HINT: Although most markets put produce away at night, you don't have to go without. Most are happy to bring out what you need if you ask politely.)

Do the same with the Laundromat. If you go early in the morning or late at night, you won't have to wait on machines or wheeled baskets. The Laundromat is so peaceful during those hours that it's also a great time to catch up on your reading, letter writing, or goal setting. The other advantage to doing laundry and shopping early is that you'll be done early—and have a full day free for more fun things.

Even if you own a washing machine, if you have several loads to do in a hurry, a Laundromat allows you to do them all—in about the same time it takes to do one load. Of course, if you wash each load as it is accumulated, it won't ever become a major task. And we've already discussed in Principle #6 how using your faithful kitchen timer can free you to do other things while your clothes wash and dry in the apartment complex laundry room.

Shop by Mail

While advanced scheduling of your local shopping increases efficiency, you can save even more time by using catalogs to shop. There are a few helpful hints that apply to catalog shopping.

First, deal only with catalogs you are familiar with and that offer high-quality products (if in doubt, ask friends for recommendations). If you receive bad service or quality from any mail-order house, send the address label back to them immediately, asking to be removed from their mailing list (see Principle #5).

Secondly, actually write up the order on the order form and date it, even if calling it in. By doing this you will have all the necessary ordering information handy when you place the call. When you finish ordering, make a note of the name of the person who took your order, and staple the order form to only those pages in the catalog on which your ordered items appear (tear out the pages and discard the bulky catalog). If you mail in your order, keep a photocopy or write up a duplicate order for your records. File the order in your pending or tickler file under the date it should arrive (see Principle #4). Now you will have contact numbers and ordering information handy if it becomes necessary to follow-up on the order. Furthermore, when you receive your goods, you will have a list to verify that you have received what you requested. Once the shipment is verified, attach the packing slip to the other paperwork in order to verify the charge when it appears on your credit card statement. After that, the paperwork can be filed in the appropriate deductible or nondeductible expense file.

Shop for gifts throughout the year and store them for birthdays and holidays. Just think of all the panic you'll remove from your life. Another advantage is that you spread expenditures out so you're not caught at year's end with a horrendous outgo of funds or credit card charges you'll be paying until the following October.

Keep extra, generic-type gifts on hand as well, for those last-minute weddings, showers, coworker or classmate birthday parties, or for a friend who needs the lift an unexpected gift can bring. If you buy unique items as they catch your eye, you'll never be caught empty-handed or have to settle for a less-than-perfect gift because you don't have time to search for it.

Use Your Entire Twenty-Four Hours

We all need to sleep, but many of us sleep too much. Unless there's an earthquake or tornado, someone's breaking into your house, or your upstairs neighbor is a night owl who likes loud music, your body usually wakes up when it's had enough rest. If your alarm hasn't gone off yet, so what? Get up anyway. You'll be amazed at what you can do with that extra hour.

Many times we sleep because we're bored, and then our bodies get used to having the extra, unnecessary sleep. If we sleep more than our bodies require, we're generally sluggish all day. So sleep enough to be alert but then get up and find excitement—or make your own.

The best way to find out your individual sleep requirement is to experiment. Set aside two or three days when you can forgo setting the alarm. Go to bed when you feel tired, get up when you wake up, making notes of the times. After a couple of days you should notice your body's natural rhythm. Now try to reorganize your daily schedule to accommodate that rhythm. More and more companies are recognizing the value of flextime or at-home offices to increase productivity. If your employer doesn't offer such, campaign for this important freedom. (HINT: If you can't regulate your work hours, turn off the TV and go to bed early, or use power naps [see Principle #6] to get the rest you need.)

Insomnia is another big time waster. Using the personal journal and/or Things-To-Do Diary suggested in Principle #4 can aid in alleviating the problem by clearing your worries from your brain before you go to bed. But if you still can't sleep, instead of tossing and turning or plotting how to kill that noisy neighbor, get up and read or complete a chore you have scheduled for the following day until you are tired enough to go back to sleep. Even if you miss some sleep, the feeling of accomplishment will revitalize you, and if you complete one of your chores, you can hopefully make up the time by sleeping a little later in the morning.

Even when you're sleeping, you can use the time constructively by dreaming. You can solve problems in your dreams. Before you go to sleep, call to mind every detail of a knotty situation. Imagine yourself asking a little person in your brain, which is really the big voice of the Great Spirit, to give you some answers in the night. It is said that Einstein did this regularly. If you poll successful individuals, most will say they practice this technique consistently. You can create in your dreams, too. I've come up with many story plots, business ideas and inventions in my dreams. Steve Allen, among others, has written songs in his dreams.

As already mentioned under Principle #3, keep a tape recorder by your bed so you can capture your dreams before you get up. The advantage of a tape recorder over a notepad (which also works, by the way) is that you don't have to turn on a light and can therefore describe your dream from your alpha state. You will remember more details that way. Many times I've played a tape back days later and cannot remember dictating— or even having—a particular dream I made note of when I was only partially awake. Be sure to record the date of the dream as well. That way if you don't have time to transcribe it into your written journal the next day, you'll still know exactly when you dreamed what.

The beauty of recording your dreams on the written page is that they are always available for reference. Also, once you get into the habit of recording your dreams, you'll begin remembering them almost every night. Since dreaming is often symbolic, having a written record to compare with actual life events can help you interpret your individual symbols. (This may be completely different from what a dream book tells you, by the way. You will know if you have discovered the correct meaning by that "Eureka!" feeling that surges up when you think of it.)

There are three other tricks to understanding what a dream means. One is to write them down in the present tense. For some reason this makes them easier to decipher. The second is to work with a friend and have them ask you questions about your dream. What does this mean to you? How do you feel about that?

The last trick is similar to this, but you can do it alone. Pretend that you are telling your dream to a little purple man from Mars and have to define each symbol in it. What is a car? It's a vehicle to take you from one place to another. What in your life is the "vehicle" that is taking you from where you are to where you are headed. What is a mouse? It's a tiny little animal that runs really fast to hide when it is afraid. Are you running and hiding from something? The context of the mouse in your dream will help you answer the what. Consider the people in your dreams a representation of a part of yourself. Ask yourself, "What trait immediately comes to mind when I think of that person?" Or think about what one adjective would best describe that person to others. Get the idea? Try this—you'll see it makes the dream much clearer.

Use Travel Time Wisely

Long drives can get monotonous, and traffic jams can make us lose our religion. But fortunately, the time spent in your vehicle does not have to be wasted. In fact, it's one of the best times to combine activities. You can memorize lines or practice a speech. You can have a heart-to-heart talk with your child, spouse, friend, or yourself. You can practice asking for a raise or promotion, or making an important sales pitch. When going on vacations to new areas, you can use driving time to brief yourself on the locale and to visualize an exciting adventure. Car phones have made it possible to conduct your business on wheels. (HINT: If you're on a busy road, however, do what my friend, comedian Blake Clark, says, "Hang up the phone and drive!")

Audiotapes are available on just about any subject you can imagine. You can "read" that classic you've always wanted to read, learn a foreign language, or focus on spiritual growth. If you don't have a tape deck or CD player in your car, carry a small portable model with you. There are so many options today you can literally turn your vehicle into a university on wheels.

You can also organize your day while you drive. If stress is plaguing your life, your car is the perfect place for "scream therapy." No one can hear you, so pretend you are vying for the lead role in a horror flick. It's deliciously effective.

If you prefer a more passive approach to stress, meditate while you drive. (Just don't go into an altered state!) There's something about being enclosed in a small space and moving down the road that frees the mind. If you carry a tape recorder with you, you can capture all kinds of ideas that might otherwise get lost in the jumble of daily activity. I once dictated an entire script while driving from Tennessee to South Texas and was amazed at how fast the trip went, even across the endless plains of Texas.

When traveling by bus, subway or train, use a portable player with headphones to do any of the things suggested above. Also, as you board, ask the driver to announce your stop. Not having to watch the streets, or worry about missing your street, frees your mind for reading, thinking, writing a letter, or planning your day. If you're familiar with the route and know how long it takes to get to your stop, carry your trusty little timer (see Principle #4) and set it for a couple of minutes before you have to get off. Or use the alarm on your watch, if you have one.

Just Do It

Long before Nike made that slogan popular, I came to the conclusion that procrastination is one of the biggest time wasters that besets mankind. Banish the phrase, "Someday I'm gonna . . ." from your vocabulary. Putting things off can turn a simple task into a horrible headache.

The monthly and daily goal setting described under Principle #2 can help prevent procrastination.

Sometimes you put off doing something because you're not quite sure how to proceed. This happens to me when I'm writing, and sometimes a period of creative gestation is necessary. The important difference between this gestation period and procrastination is that during the delay my brain continues to explore solutions while I go about my other tasks or even while I sleep. The same gestation period may be necessary before you write that important proposal for your employer or prepare for the party you want to have. If you come up with an approach to a problem and don't try it, however, you've slipped over into the trap of procrastination.

Think about this: Procrastination is fear. If you are procrastinating about something, keep asking why to your every justification and eventually, if you are truly honest, you will boil your reason for procrastinating down to fear. Once you have identified the fear, you can resolve it—or at least accept it—and you will be able to move on.

We all have the same number of minutes in every day. How we use them determines how organized and how successful we are.

Energy flow for natural task achievement:

_____

_____

_____

_____

_____

_____

_____

_____

_____

_____

Know contentment
And you will suffer no disgrace;
Know when to stop
And you will meet with no danger.
You can then endure.

True
success
is being
happy.

Principle Ten: Relax...have fun

The whole point of being organized is to be able to enjoy life more. If we don't look at life as a fun adventure, what's the point of having more time to live it? We need to organize our time to include nights out at the theater, tennis, bowling, visiting with friends and the like. We should plan quiet times at home to daydream or pamper ourselves and time for the stimulation of a good workout or walk. But this principle is more about finding enjoyment in everything we do, including those tasks we truly dread. Here are some helpful ideas to make those tasks, maybe not fun but at least more pleasant.

Dress Appropriately

If you tried to change the oil in your car in your best business suit and had to worry about grease stains, you would not be able to get the job done very quickly, right? Well, that same rule applies in everything you do. If you are going to be cleaning out files, storage areas, or the oven, dress in clothes you don't have to worry about, in clothes that are comfortable-so you don't have to waste another moment of thought on your wardrobe. If you're cleaning the shower, do it naked. If you're washing the car, wear a bathing suit. If you want to be the life of the party, dress in sparkling clothes that fit your mood. If you want to make an impression of strength and professionalism, a basic suit immediately sets the tone.

Always dress to feel comfortable and confident. When you pick out your outfit, visualize doing whatever it is you're about to do. Even if you don't see the actual clothes you're wearing, at least this allows you to list in your head the requirements of the clothes that will best fit the action. Clothes should make you so comfortable wearing them that you don't have to think about them again.

Remember the time you went to a party and had to continually worry about your belt riding up in back, your too-short shirt coming untucked, or a button coming open because the hole was too loose? Imagine every way in which your clothes might distract you from the planned activity and do your best to eliminate those pesky problems by reselecting or repairing. And don't forget comfortable shoes. If your feet hurt, you will constantly lose your focus on—and enjoyment of—any situation.

Consider colors, too. Colors have been proven to affect our moods. Wear red if you want to be bold, darker colors if you want to be serious, bright colors for a party mood. Black can make you feel elegant, white will make you feel innocent, and yellow will put you in a happy, childlike frame of mind. Consider purple when you want to feel classy, orange for sexy, green if you're in a moneymaking mood. Pink augments healing and love, and blue inspires creativity. Use all the colors to support your mood.

Use Music

I don't understand the science of it—I think it has something to do with the vibrational rates of the tones—but music sets a mood better than almost anything. If you have to clean the house, up-tempo music, as already mentioned in Principle #5, will definitely make the work go faster because your body automatically gets into the peppy rhythm. Suppose you want to focus on a complex report, do your income taxes, or complete another assignment that requires concentration. Soft instrumentals or environmental tapes (sounds of ocean waves, summer storms, babbling brooks) can help you accomplish the task more quickly by drowning out outside noises and helping you relax. For many people, classical music is inspirational. Recent studies also show that classical music actually improves mental capabilities and concentration.

For putting inspirational thoughts on paper, choose music that provides enough mellowness to eliminate stress but enough punch so that you don't get too relaxed to get things done. This music may also work well for driving, to keep you alert but considerate on the road. Instrumental jazz is also a great perker-upper that doesn't infringe on your concentration.

If you're unable to play recorded music while you work, make your own. Whistle, hum or sing out loud. However, when playing music, please consider those around you. They may prefer a different type of music or none at all, so don't force your preferences on them by blasting up the volume. Headphones are inexpensive and should be used as necessary to honor others' space.

Be Creative

Play improvisational games to teach yourself how to think creatively, which is one of the primary keys to being organized. Watch comedians like Robin Williams and Gallagher perform, and then try it yourself. Collect some props and see how many ways you can think of to use them. Make it a family affair. Hold up a paper plate and see who can come up with the most ways to use it. Or not to use it!

Another fun exercise to help you learn to think creatively is to make a list of ten random objects (nouns) down the left side of a piece of paper. Now cover these and forget about them. Call to mind a particular occupation and list down the center of the paper ten verbs that apply to that occupation, one per line opposite the nouns that you wrote earlier. (HINT: When making both lists, write down the first words that pop into your thoughts.) Remove the paper covering the listed nouns and write a sentence using each set of noun and verb. This game can put a whole new twist on a familiar word and free your brain to view other, unrelated things in a new light.

There is also a game called Mad-Libs that involves basically the same principle, only a complete story is created by slotting random nouns, verbs or adjectives into preprinted text. This is just one of many games that can help develop creativity while they contribute to the enjoyment of your family and friends.

If you get in the habit of looking at things creatively and considering less common functions for everyday items, your schedule will be less likely to be thrown off by lack of proper tools to complete a task.

Remember the Child

Have you ever noticed how children get joy out of everything they do? The next time you have an odious task to complete—cleaning the tub and shower is one of mine—try imagining how a child, encountering it for the first time, would view that activity. Make it into a game. On an episode of the TV show "The Simpsons," Bart had to miss a school field trip because he had forgotten his permission slip. The principal gave him envelopes to lick to keep him busy and suggested that Bart make a game of it by counting how many he licked in an hour and then trying to do more in the next hour. Try something like that.

Remember the family trips you took as a child? You would play games to pass the time—finding the alphabet in order on the billboards, seeing license plates from other states. Maybe such things don't get you to your destination any faster, but they certainly keep you alert and make the trip seem shorter. Another traveling game is really a psychic exercise. Think of a question: What color will the next car I encounter be? What is the name of the next restaurant that will be advertised? What three letters or numbers will be on the next license plate I will see? Now relax and let the information just enter your head. Your logical mind will try to make a guess based on odds. Ignore that and focus on the answer that floats into your consciousness unbidden. Over time you'll notice you'll have more and more correct guesses, and the benefits of your new awareness will filter over into other areas of your life as well.

We all have tremendous psychic abilities and their benefit to our efficiency and organizational skills is obvious, so seize every opportunity to avail yourself of this powerful gift.

In addition to inspiring creativity, childish props are good for letting off steam. Use a rubber fish or chicken, a laugh box, Groucho glasses, or a paper noisemaker to bring a laugh and banish a bad mood. Or look in the mirror as you sing a silly childhood tune, complete with gestures. Skip around in circles as you sing. If you don't want to sing, make faces at yourself in the mirror. If you want to feel really delicious, do this someplace where you might get caught, like the office bathroom. Who knows, maybe the person who catches you is in need of a laugh and you will be doing hir a favor!

Plan Rewards

Rewards worked when we were young and they still work as adults. Just can't seem to get yourself motivated to clean the refrigerator, or your toolbox, or a file cabinet at work? Set a deadline to have it completed and then plan a celebration: "If I get the laundry done by noon on Saturday, I will go hiking in the mountains all afternoon"; "If I complete this report by 4:00, I will go to the beach and watch the sunset."

Visualize the results of your labors. The pride of accomplishment is sometimes enough reward in itself, although a bubble bath or a good bottle of champagne or chilled apple cider can never hurt.

Find a Hobby

If you feel bogged down by your workload, maybe it's because you have not found a way for your creative self to express itself. When you have a rare day off, do you spend it in the same old rut of catching up with chores or sleeping? Maybe you just wander around trying to decide what to do. You need a hobby.

Think of something that gives you pleasure. A stroll in the park or the country looking for birds, bicycling, drawing with crayons, washing and waxing your car until it shines, writing your biography or obituary (now that'll make you think about what's important!), painting (even if by number), gardening, photography, doing needlepoint, cooking a gourmet meal. How about putting together model airplanes or building elaborate structures with Legos? It doesn't matter if you're good at this hobby. It only matters if it makes you happy.

If you have many hobbies you'd like to at least try, but you never seem to have enough time to do them all, or if, when you do have a free hour or two, you can't decide which to do first, make up a hobby jar. As ideas occur to you—and they usually pop up in conversations with yourself or others in the form of, "Someday I'd like to . . ."—write them on a small piece of scratch paper, fold it up, and put it in a jar. Now when free time pops up, draw one out and do it. Better yet, carve out at least an hour each week to draw a project from the jar and indulge. (HINT: This same idea works great for children who complain about being bored. You can even add little jobs they are capable of doing. If they know that if they don't entertain themselves you'll draw an activity for them, you'll be amazed at how many fewer times you'll hear, "Mom, there's nothing to do.")

Eliminate Stress

Calmness is crucial to being organized. When we are stressed out, we spin our wheels. It's the old chicken-with-his-head-cut-off syndrome. Even if we do get everything on our list done, we're usually too wrung out to enjoy the time left in our day. Worse, continued stress can cause illness. There are many things you can do every day to break up the stress that threatens to take over. Here are just a few ideas.

Acknowledge your uniqueness. Lavish yourself with flowers. A single rose to gaze at and smell throughout the day cannot fail to bring a smile, the ultimate stress buster. Have a colorful spring bouquet or potted plant delivered to yourself at work. If you're not a flower person, try a singing telegram, or a bouquet of balloons, or mail yourself a clever card.

Use props. Remind yourself of your uniqueness. Buy a Far Side calendar, display a favorite gift from a friend or a mug purchased on your vacation, or frame a picture of the pet that gives you unconditional love. A quick glance at the object may be all you need to get relief.

Take a brisk walk. Walking frees the mind and the spirit. If the weather's bad, use the halls and stairways. Going up and down stairs is marvelous cardiovascular exercise and a real pick-me-up.

Take a break. Sit back for five minutes. If you can lie down somewhere, even better. This includes at work. Maybe you can talk your employer into providing a quiet area and a padded slant board. The increased productivity from a five-minute break under these conditions will more than repay the cost. Using a sleep mask will make five minutes feel like ten. Don't forget to use your timer (see Principle #6) for complete relaxation.

Take a mind trip. Take three deep breaths and close your eyes. Imagine yourself at the ocean, in the desert, riding a horse, climbing a mountain, in a hot spring with the person of your dreams, being a cat. Doing anything you want to do. Be careful . . . if your thoughts are Xrated, your smile may betray you!

Call your travel agent or get on the Internet and get airline information to anywhere you'd like to go. You don't have to buy the ticket; just pretending you're going is usually enough to lift you from the doldrums.

If you can't close your eyes or get on the Internet, just stare at your computer screen or your textbook or whatever, and see the vision play out in your mind's eye. Your trusty timer will remind you to go back to work.

Use scents to cheer you up. There's a reason why aromatherapy is so popular: It works. Try burning some of the following herbs with incense, using them in sachet form in your drawers or linens, or even in your bath. (HINT: Putting herbs into a ball-type tea strainer makes for easy cleanup of the tub.) Try rosemary for mental stimulation; red clover for calmness; thyme for good health; alfalfa to prevent poverty or help arthritis; lavender for love; and marjoram for nervousness. This is just a short list, but it can get you started. There are many books on the subject if you want to investigate aromatherapy further.

Grab a book. When the day starts to jangle, read a page from a poetry book or book of inspirational sayings. Fairy tales and Greek mythology are also good for taking your mind beyond problems to that space of peace.

Get the kinks out. Close your eyes. Bend your head slowly downward until your chin touches your chest. Hold for a count of ten. Return your head to the upright position. Lean your head back as far as it will go for the count of ten. Return. Now slowly attempt to touch your right ear to your right shoulder. If it helps, place your right hand on top of your head, and gently pull toward your shoulder. Don't strain. Hold for ten. Left ear to left shoulder for ten.

Keeping your eyes level, turn your head, slowly, to look as far behind your right shoulder as you can. Now face slowly forward. Now, slowly look over your left shoulder. Return.

Raise your arms in the air, clasping your hands together. Stretch them as far upward as you can. Now slowly bend your right elbow and bring it down to your side so that your left arm rests across the top of your head. Hold for 10, then do it in the opposite direction.

Okay, back to work.

This is just one of the many quick and easy exercises you can do to banish the stress that tightens your muscles. Magazines, books, t'ai chi and yoga instruction manuals are excellent places to find those that work best for you. Many can be done anytime and any place, so do them as often as necessary.

Courtesy counts. Smile at five people you don't know. Notice how many times this brings a return smile. Notice how it makes you feel, even if the other person doesn't respond. Say "please" and "thank you" to everyone. Help someone out, if at all possible. Smile at someone across the room at a party—yes, even your spouse.

The good feeling courtesy gives us automatically makes us more efficient because it gives value to the seconds of the day that make up our individual lives.

Marvel at life's mysteries. "Why?" and "How?" are two favorite questions of toddlers that we somehow forget to ask ourselves as we grow older. For a great stress buster, put them back into active service in your life. Stare out the window and ask yourself things like: Why does the sky change color? What do clouds feel like? Why is that mountain shaped just the way it is? How in the world does a seed know how to grow? How did that hole get in that tree? How do birds know when to fly north and south? How do dogs find their way back home over thousands of miles?

With so many mysteries in life, can you really get so bent out of shape by a typewriter ribbon that winds incorrectly, snow that needs shoveling, or the high-power meeting at noon? Use the wonders of life to banish stress.

Count your blessings. Visit a hospital emergency room, children's burn unit, cancer or AIDS patient areas, or a home for the elderly. Does your own situation still seem so problematic?

Eat, drink and be merry. Sip a cup of chamomile or dandelion tea. Eat some chocolate. Splurge at lunch.

Breathe. Learn yoga breathing techniques, which are opposite of how the Western world breathes. Extend your stomach as you inhale, slowly letting it cave in as your lungs fill. Now, contract your stomach muscles as you exhale through your mouth. It is one of the fastest and, once you've retrained yourself, easiest way to allow stress to float away on a cloud of nothingness. (HINT: Yoga breathing is also wonderful for relieving hot flashes during menopause.)

Daydream. Look out a window. Focus on a tree, cloud, pigeon, squirrel, butterfly, or other wild creature until you almost seem to become one with it and nature. Imagine being whatever you see. What are you thinking? How does it feel to float across space like a bird? To wave in the wind like a branch? To have elevators cruise up and down your side like that skyscraper? To hammer your beak into a tree? Nature is so incredible, just contemplating it banishes stress.

Pat yourself on the back. Sit back and relish the feeling of accomplishment for a job well done, or even for living and learning as many years as you have. Congratulate yourself for doing something even so commonplace as getting out of bed this morning or not burning the toast.

Love yourself. You are perfect just the way you are because any Being who can hang the stars and start the planets rotating cannot make junk.

Allow yourself to be less organized in some areas of life if it will help you be more organized in others. I used to beat myself up terribly about things. I always thought I had to be doing something to improve my lot in life. I would rant and rave to my friend John David Carson, "What should I do? I don't know what to do!" John would simply say, "You don't have to do anything, you just have to be." It took me a while to understand what he was saying, to appreciate the wisdom of his words, which is essentially the Tao philosophy. But now, finally allowing myself just to be, like nature just is, has changed my life by allowing me to love myself just the way I am. And, as with Tao, everything still manages to get done, usually better than before.

Be grateful. After hearing Oprah rave about the benefits of keeping a gratitude journal (from Sarah Ban Breathnach's inspirational book *Simple Abundance*, Warner Books, 1995), I decided to give it a try. Oprah is right. It is life-changing!. A gratitude journal is nothing more than a small notebook in which you write down five things daily for which you are grateful. Keeping such a journal opens one up to the incredible blessing of every moment we are given. Even on bad days most of us can at least put down having a roof over our heads, nourishing food on our table, good health, that we're not at war, and that—always—we have free will to choose to be and do anything we want. I urge you to try it. It is a wonderful tool for learning to appreciate life as it is.

Get Excited

Every successful person knows the value of the adage: "If you act as if, then you will be." Try looking at a mundane task as the most exciting thing you've ever tackled. Laugh about it. Talk about how much fun it will be to delve into the project. Anticipate it as you do an upcoming party. Start doing this a couple of days before you actually have to begin the assignment so that by the time you undertake it, you're already convinced it'll be a snap. You'll be amazed at how fast you'll breeze through even the most ponderous job.

Learn to Laugh

Studies show that a four-year-old child laughs up to 500 times a day compared to the average adult who laughs about fifteen times a day. We need to change those statistics. Laughter is the most precious gift we have been given for coping with life. If you don't believe me, try this experiment:

For the next twenty-one days, when you wake up in the morning, before you get out of bed, laugh. I mean a good, long belly laugh. Hold your sides and think of the funniest thing you ever saw or heard—and laugh some more.

Now keep that smile resting easy on your lips all day. When things start to annoy you, make yourself laugh. If your life doesn't go more smoothly than ever before, I want to know about it.

Even if you don't accomplish everything you set out to do in the day, you will have had fun, so what does it really matter in the big scheme of things?

When work is getting you down, or the kids, or just life in general, acknowledge your stress and then laugh. Think of every irritation as a funny story to tell and laugh some more.

If you're having trouble jump-starting your laughter, here are a few tricks to get you going.

Write down at least five funny things that happen every day. Clip cartoons and post them up on your refrigerator, your bedroom mirror, a file cabinet, or a bulletin board. I cut out comic strips that make me laugh out loud and paste them into an inexpensive, oversized scrapbook. If I'm blue or spinning my wheels, a few minutes spent skimming through these pages brings at least a smile. Rent a comedy video, listen to a comedy audiotape, or watch Comedy Central on TV. Imagine your life being acted out or talked about in these forums. Laugh.

He who knows others
is clever;
He who knows himself
has discernment.
He who overcomes others
has force;
He who overcomes himself
is strong.
He who knows contentment
is rich;
He who perseveres
is a man of purpose;
He who does not lose his station
will endure;
He who lives out his days
has had a long life.

*You are
doing exactly
what you have
chosen to do.
If you're not
happy, make a
new choice!*

Summary

Okay, so you've read through the book. Now it is time for action. The first thing to do is to remember that clutter did not fill your mind and your life overnight, and it will not dissipate just because you read this book and want it to. As with anything else you want to master, you must make a commitment to practice.

Start small. Pick only one or two ideas you think will adapt to your lifestyle and make it easier and more fun to live.

Now, make a commitment to practice these selected routines for the next twenty-one days. If you falter, pick yourself up and go on. If you find yourself asking, "What's the point?", answer, "Because I have made a commitment and I honor my commitments."

Remember the Tao of finding the path of least resistance to change.

If at the end of twenty-one days your new habits have not made a positive difference in your life, revise or abandon them. Try another idea. Honoring your commitment will still have benefited your soul.

MORNING AFFIRMATION
Today I act efficiently.

I WILL. . . .
Imagine
Plan Ahead
Keep Things Simple
Write Things Down
Use Assembly-Line Principles
Use Time Saving Devices
Develop Teamwork
Develop Harmonious Habits
Honor Time
Relax . . . Have Fun!

EVENING AFFIRMATION
Today I acted efficiently. Tomorrow I will be even more organized.

In closing, my wish for you is this: May you discover at least one idea in this book to make your life run more smoothly and may you always carry a smile in your heart.
Now . . .

DO IT NOW

When Your Life is Organized...
You will have:

Less Anger,More Smile
Less Worry, More Sleep
Less Speaking, More Doing
Less Desire, More Service
Less Food, More Energy
Less Sweet, More Natural
Less Brine, More Vinegar
Less Meat, More Vegetables
Less Mess, More Time
Less Pavement, More Path

Source: East-North Corner Chi Gong Institute

Printed in the United States
34329LVS00006B/136-156

9 780893 342937